Toward a Male Spirituality

For
Bill Barry

Third printing 1991

Twenty-Third Publications
185 Willow Street
P.O. Box 180
Mystic, CT 06355
(203) 536-2611
800-321-0411

ISBN 0-89622-410-4
Library of Congress Catalog Card Number 89-50905

Preface

This book had its beginnings in the presentations made at the Villanova University Theology Institute in June 1987. The overall topic of that Institute was "A Discipleship of Equals: Toward a Christian Feminist Spirituality." My assignment was to reflect on what a spirituality for men might look like in such a context.

Partly in admiration for what I have taken to be women's predilection for the personal over the abstract, and partly from my own convictions about the essentials of a viable spirituality, my presentations tended to use the first person singular. If such a choice needs to be defended now that I am addressing a wider audience, I would say that my judgment has been that women's spirituality owes the great strides it has made in recent years to its insistence that experience, rather than a priori expectations, supposedly normative patterns, or sexual stereotypes, ought to dominate what people say about their deepest views of God, themselves, one another, and the love brought front and center by all three of the relationships these terms imply.

I also believe that spirituality differs from theology in that it is more obviously existential—so much a matter of experiences, feelings, and deep judgments that what usually pass as "data" and "scholarship" manifestly are secondary, though of course significant, considerations. One might argue similarly for the personalizing of theology, and I would support much of such an argument, but the case for detachment, objectivity, and scholarship in theological matters is strong and the rights of the academy are potent. Not many theologians, Catholic or Protestant, are willing to treat theology as personally and existentially as the late Karl Rahner did, and so few are able to fold speculative and pastoral theology into one another as dexterously as he.

At any rate, regardless of the outcome of debates one might develop on these matters, I will attempt here to be concrete and personal. That means, of course, that I am more interested in having readers muse about what I propose and consider its analogies in their own lives than I am in laying down hard and fast guidelines. My own spirit has taken wing whenever I've read or heard that only the Holy Spirit can teach us to pray or make us wise according to the mind of Christ.

Trying to discern what this implies, I have decided that part of our birthright as children of God is the freedom to tailor traditional advice to our own personalities and circumstances. Love may apply always and everywhere, but what love means here and now, or the primary designs love ought to develop through a given person's days, can vary considerably. So my hope is that the stories I tell and the reflections I put forward mainly will help other men, and women, better feel the touch of God's Spirit in their own lives. To that end, I have tried to speak from my own struggles and hopes, trusting that readers will give me the benefit of their sympathy and good humor as well as their doubts.

My thanks to Rev. Francis A. Eigo, O.S.A., Director of The Villanova University Theology Institute, both for inviting me to participate in the 1987 session and for granting permission to use the materials I presented there in this book. My thanks, as well, to Maria Harris and Mary Jo Weaver, with whom I shared a half-week of mutual criticism at the Institute, and to Joann Wolski Conn, Mary Ann Getty, and Constance Fitzgerald (the troika for the other halfweek), whose papers I read with great profit. My friends William A. Barry, S.J., and Felicidad Oberholzer read my paper and offered helpful comments. My wife, Denise Lardner Carmody, provided good cautions and wonderful support, as is her wont. Finally, my thanks to Stephen Scharper of Twenty-Third Publications for suggesting the transformation of my paper into a book and shepherding it through publication.

Contents

Introduction

Usually I do not pay much attention to my dreams. Years ago I read Freud and Jung, and the unflattering dream about the church that Jung mentions in his autobiography has long amused me, but normally I do not consider my dreams a theological source. But early in the morning of the day I was to begin writing this book, I had a beautiful dream, a dream so strong and winning that I had to take it seriously. That day I had planned to discover what I wanted to say by working on my first draft. I had hoped in that way to resolve my ambivalence about my topic: did I think there was a spirituality distinctively for men? After the dream I realized I thought my book should be about love, with more explicit attention to my male voice than usually I pay it.

1

ambivalence about my topic. It stems from my dislike of dis-junctive treatments of sexuality. I think men and women have differences, but that these differences should weigh less than what they hold in common. I think that each of us goes to God as a unique individual, shaped by genes, sex, family upbringing, social conditioning, education, and the gifts of a Holy Spirit who is not a generic Paraclete, but a Comforter treating us as distinc-tive individuals she could no more abandon than her nursing children. And, I find that the best community, the richest expe-rience of romance, work, friendship, and communal prayer all flourish when we attend to the concrete, individual whole that any person standing beside us is and chasten our tendency to perceive or react through stereotypes.

Consequently, I find myself slow to pick up books about male bonding, columns especially for men, invitations to join men's groups. These things embarrass me and, after I have admitted that some such embarrassment might be a good thing, a way of learning more about myself and other men, I find part of my re-sistance salutary. I do not want advice and preoccupation that set men over against women, that do not from the outset distin-guish only to unite. Equally, I am put off by women's writing that is separatist. I read quite a lot of feminist literature and the-ology, partly because I share an interest of my wife Denise and partly because I find much of it highly instructive. One of the things I have most admired about Doris Lessing, Margaret At-wood, Mary Gordon, Rosemary Ruether, Monika Hellwig, and many other women writers is their realism. They accept a two-sexed world. The graces they celebrate and the sins they de-plore cut across stereotypes. With Dorothy Dinnerstein, they agree that the sexual malaise we suffer is a product of both sex-es' collaboration. Sometimes they are hard on men, but almost always with good reason. I myself tend to be harder on men, thinking that real men take no pleasure in hurting women.[2]

Part One

The Love of God

$\backsim$ 1 $\sim$

Loving the One God

MY DIVISION OF THIS PART OWES A
debt to the scholastic distinction of the tracts *De Deo Uno* and *De
Deo Trino*. It reflects, as well, some study of Judaism, Islam, and
the theology of nature. From time immemorial, people have enjoyed moments when the world showed itself as the material
face of an intriguing, almost crushingly beautiful mystery. Like
many an Eskimo, the naturalist Barry Lopez has recently re-
sponded to the beauty of the Arctic with praise verging on religious poetry:

> I remember the press of light against my face, the explosive
> skitter of calves among grazing caribou. And the warm in-
> tensity of the eggs beneath these resolute birds. Until then,
> perhaps because the sun was still shining in the very mid-

7

dle of the night, so out of tune with my own customary
perception, I had never known how benign sunlight could
be. How forgiving. How run through with compassion in
a land that bore so eloquently the evidence of centuries of
winter.[3]

My spirituality for men would have a bigger place for love of
the one God manifested in such natural beauty than did the
spirituality I was taught. For personal as well as ecological reasons, I want to recapture the intimacy with the Lord of the
Worlds, the Great Goddess of Life, that Muslims and Hindus, in
their very different ways, have experienced. By virtue of the
Christian understanding of creation and grace, men might experience the fields they tramp, the oceans they sail, as charged
with the grandeur of God. They might nod with approval when
preachers remind them that the biblical God is never captured
by nature and always remains transcendent, yet reserve their
heartier accord for those who claim that any fall of a cherry blos-
som might trigger enlightenment. One has only to dabble in
present-day science—the physics of a Stephen Hawking or the
neurology of an Oliver Sacks—to be staggered by the profusion
of nature, the sweep and intricacy of the world. Job had his Be-
hemoth and Leviathan. Men of today should read the natural
signs of our times as Job's world to the nth power. For faith, our
world should seem a constant series of theophanies. One has
only to think about what is there to admire what happens, to
magnify the power of the one God, to minimize all human hu-
bris, and to wonder, most profoundly, what we human beings
are, that God should care for us.

For present purposes, I am not much interested in the theodi-
cy that a fully adequate treatment probably would enter at this
point. Nature, like human culture, does present suffering,
waste, and destruction that make questions about the existence
and goodness of God legitimate, even necessary. Moreover,
these questions can persist within faith, always speaking up for
the rights of atheists, always cautioning us not to get glib or sac-

charine. Our science is different from the science of Boethius's day, so our declarations that providence always orchestrates things for the best has to be similarly different. Yet, ultimately, we should be able to say that the wisdom of God justifies creation. And, frequently, we should remind ourselves that the profusion of goodness is at least as mysterious as the profusion of evil. Our regular memo to ourselves should be that we come from nothing and have no rights God has not bestowed upon us. Our regular prayer should be thanksgiving that we, and many other human beings, have enjoyed lives that make it relatively easy to say amen to divine providence, relatively easy to agree that God was good to have given us the light of our eyes and the air we breathe.

Another way of proposing this attitude that I would like men to develop toward the one God, the maker of heaven and earth, is by waxing ontological. Matthew Fox and others interested in a spirituality that pays as much attention to creation as to redemption have revived the convictions of the medieval mystics about panentheism. God is in us and we are in God. The medieval mystics (and any who, like them, find existence wonderful) meant this physically. That we are is more primordial than what we are. That God exists is more certain than what God is. Our culture generally has lost the contemplative orientation that makes such assertions significant. We rush and bustle amid concrete and neon, losing our ties with the quiet of early morning, when being seems fresh like dew, with the quiet of late night, when unknowing clearly is the way to a good night's sleep.

I realize, of course, that monks and some nuns keep the contemplative rhythms. Most of the men I meet, however, find talk of contemplation less intelligible than Sanskrit. Indeed, they find it suspect: inimical to the pragmatism regnant in their worlds of business and education and so, subversive.

Recently, I reviewed James V. Schall's *The Distinctiveness of Christianity*.[4] It struck me as a piece of nostalgia, built on theses of G. K. Chesterton, Christopher Dawson, and other names I had not much seen for at least a decade. John Paul II was another prime source. Schall spoke pejoratively of justice, as though liberation theologians had made it the enemy of charity. He lamented the demise of Catholic higher education, charging that most American Catholic schools had sold their birthright for a bowl of secularism. He had little space for women, minorities, and the statistical realities of poverty around our globe. In most ways his book was a prime example of Catholic triumphalism.

And yet, I loved the book. For its good style, its author's humanity (he always stayed on the near side of shrillness and vitriol), its call for a return to epistemological realism, and its devotion to contemplating the trinitarian mysteries, I was ready to forgive it the many sins that made it hopeless as a contemporary theology. It made me realize how hungry I was for the thought that had nourished me in the seminary. I was disappointed that Schall had not followed Karl Rahner and Eric Voegelin, whom he quoted several times, and Bernard Lonergan, whom he ignored, into a sublation of classical Catholic realism, its supplement by the positive aspects of the modern turn to subjectivity and empirical data. Yet, I still was moved and pacified by his Augustinian premise that God is the great treasure of human existence, that we are made to contemplate God and will have no rest until we rest in God.

The Catholic Christian vision of God as the mystery evoked in every decent luring of the human spirit seems more eloquent to me today than it has ever been. I am happy enough to see men cluster in groups to discuss the alienations caused by the inhuman pace of much of today's work. I admit that relations with women have been greatly complicated by the women's movement, herpes, AIDS, the economic depression afflicting the middle of the country, and maybe even sunspots. If men find it helpful to discuss these things, with or without basketball or bowling, fine and dandy. But I myself am looking for a few good men with whom to discuss my shabby prayer, my forgetfulness of God's gifts, the relations between love and contemplation, the problems of getting religious experience into academically acceptable prose, the religious implications of my first significant appreciations of aging and thus mortality, my emotional distance from the Vatican shenanigans I read about in *The National Catholic Reporter*, and my feeling that I am a man without a country, at home neither in academics nor in my local Catholic diocese, which interests me as little as I interest it.

The one God, the God common to all human experience as its basal mystery, seems to have clouded my mind, to have rattled my compass, and I would like to learn from my betters, from those who are better lovers, what this strange semi-disablement means. To date it mainly has meant keeping my own counsel, wondering why I still seem quite cheerful, thinking about de Caussade and other consoling writers I enjoyed nearly thirty years ago, thinking about Nietzsche, Tibetan gurus, Hammarskjold, and others turned upside down and inside out. If there is one God, everything changes with shifts in one's relationship to him or her or it. I think men's spirituality, and women's spirituality, ought to be dealing with this, although, of course, usually not through formal, structured speeches. If it were doing its job, our spirituality would be creating many informal occasions, would be knitting together many friendships, in which sharing one's tears and fears, one's hopes and doubts, would be natural, regular, almost unthinking.

Let me specify the potential impact of appreciating the beclouding presence of the one God by ruminating about the idols—work, alcohol, consumerism, pornography, and more—that mottle so many men's lives. The one God who is the maker of heaven and earth is not in competition with our decent, proper use of any creatures. Both we and all the other creatures come from this one God, so in God's eyes there is no strife among us. We all ought to praise God, letting God love us and continue to bless us, by acting according to our best instincts. Catholic theology has long said that grace builds on these instincts, perfecting them. The problem, catalogued by the biblical writers as "idolatry," is that we easily lose perspective, lose our sense of God's overriding presence, and so fixate on something less than God. This something less can be our selves, with their so many vanities and anxieties, or it can be something external that we think will make us happy and help us shine.

The man who makes work the be all and end all of his life, to the detriment not only of his family but also of his prayer and service to God, has fallen into this pathetic trap. Although work done carefully and lovingly, honoring either the demands of one's craft or the needs of the people one is serving, rises to God as proof of God's wisdom in making beings in the divine image, work done mainly to gain extra money (beyond what a decent standard of living requires), or status, or power, twists the worker and before long brings spiritual ugliness, a warped character. The same with alcohol, drugs, an addiction to buying and accumulating, a fixation on sexual gratification. Imbalanced use of any creature makes it an instrument of sin, of alienation from God, diminishing and warping us by blocking out the source of our selfhood, the one God.

The clouding of our minds that casts all the pseudo-clarities of distorted work, sensual gratification, and pathetic striving for peer applause into doubt therefore is a divine healing. For those who keep trying to pray, even as badly as I do, such beclouding slowly makes it clear that God is not a thing. Because God is not a thing, but rather the foundation and horizon that makes all things exist, we can never grasp God. Rather, we have to stop the grasping of our minds, let our deeper spirits wave out toward God rather formlessly, and hope that God will grasp us. More likely, God will touch us lightly now and then, moving us toward a freedom, a peace, a carelessness, a warmth or love that we can't name or explain but simply know is good. When this happens, all the creatures we are tempted to idolize stand forth in their proper limitation. We see the folly of trying to add a cubit to our height or status by killing ourselves at work. We feel the self-ruin latent in our excessive drinking, eating, pursuit of sexual pleasure, concern for clothes and possessions. How we look, what others think, whether we will prosper in financial or social terms all become secondary. For the blessed moment, we are like the lilies of the field, good in our simple being, not having to toil or strive.

And, afterwards, it is a little easier, for awhile, to work and eat and buy in balanced fashion. It is a little easier to remember our origin in nothingness, and our goal of death and life with God. Certainly the fruits of prayer, the healings of the clouding given us by God's Spirit, tend to drop away, especially if we don't keep trying to reach out to God, to open our hearts and let ourselves be loved. Certainly our sin will keep most of us impure, fettered by at least mild vices, right to the end. But something immensely freeing will have begun, and with it a surprising joy. We are not what we eat, what we wear, what we earn, what others think of us. We are the possibility, the potential, the humble yet wonderful creature of God brought into focus and warmed from the core by a force, a most gentle power, that we cannot see or grasp or name or deny, a force that has given us the best moments of our lives, the times we knew why Genesis says that God looked on our creation and called it very good.

∽ 2 ∾

Christk

FOR THE FURTHER REFINEMENTS OF
the love of God brought by Christian belief in God's triune
character, I begin with Jesus the Christ. In Edward Schillebeeckx's term, he is the sacrament of our encounter with God.
This is congenial to Rahnerian theology, too, for Rahner finds Jesus to be God's eschatological Word of salvation. These could
be triumphalist notions, of course, but certainly neither of these
theologians makes them such. Both Schillebeeckx and Rahner
are sufficiently religious to leave their readers thinking that, far
from providing simple answers to the mystery of existence, Jesus deepens its wonder. Life is not a puzzle we shall solve. God
is not an equation we shall balance. Jesus is not a cipher break-
ing a code that non-Christians continue to find meaningless.

15

In discussing Christian faith, Avery Dulles promotes the image of discipleship.[5] Jesus continues to be the main priest, prophet, king, and other traditional metaphors. Dulles is not out to deny the Pantokrator or the head of the mystical body, but he is searching for something nearer, dearer, more enticing. He is verging on Loyola's notion of comradeship with Jesus, although without the military overtones.

How should men, in particular, relate today to the God-man Jesus? What might the studies of bonding, friendship, work relations, and the rest suggest? I realized recently, though not for the first time, that most of my interactions with other men are pleasant but either functional or superficial. I like a great many men, but only with a very few does the prospect of our being together gladden my heart. When that does occur, I realize that male friendship should be more like male-female enjoyment and play than I customarily assume. Perhaps an example will help.

I went to the doctor this winter to have a wart removed from my sole—not so exciting a prospect as going to the dentist, but in the same ballpark. Because of personnel shifts in our Health Maintenance Organization plan (a story about I-Thou and I-It relationships well worth discussing in some other context), I did not know the doctor who would treat me. He knocked on the door of the examining room, came in, and introduced himself. I judged him about 35, perhaps 5'7", 135 pounds, very trim, with dark blond hair, a short beard, and clear blue eyes. In three minutes I was convinced he was the born healer we all wish our doctor would be. He did not call himself Dr. Shultz and me John, as the folksy, patronizing local tradition encourages, and he didn't wear a silly three-quarter length white coat. He was soft-spoken, gentle, and respectful. I was intrigued, so I asked him a few questions, to prolong and deepen the interaction. This led to my giving him some advice about cardiovascular exercise on a NordicTrack—imagine, a doctor interested in exercise! When I left, after barely ten minutes, I wished we could be friends. I had loved the healing touch that had gone out from him, much as many disciples must have loved the touch and voice of Jesus.

I am sure that many good devotional books about Jesus promote this sort of love, although I seldom go near them. From time to time I have thought about the beloved disciple reclining on Jesus' breast and about Jesus weeping over Lazarus. But despite lengthy indoctrinations in the splendors of the devotion to the Sacred Heart, and good advice in books by people like my friend Bill Barry about speaking frankly and intimately with "the Lord," I do not often pray or think in these terms. Jesus has not been my friend and, ever since I heard a group of elderly Methodist men singing from their Protestant hymnal, "He walks with me and he talks with me and he tells me I am his own," I have squirmed at treating him that way. And yet, of course, Jesus has not called us servants but friends. He has disclosed to us, whom spiritual reading of the gospels makes his contemporaries, the things in his heart. Presumably, he is interested in the things in our hearts, all theologoumena about his already knowing them notwithstanding.

Occasionally I have thought that discipleship ought to mean fascination with Jesus, response to his beauty and goodness, perhaps even rollicking laughter at the wit that the New Testament (a less than fully Jewish book) chooses to ignore. I have thought that female disciples ought to respond to Jesus as a very attractive man and that male disciples ought to respond to Jesus as a very attractive man, with all the implications that this term ought to carry in the two different cases. I have enjoyed times with male friends (especially in the early years of the seminary, when we were free to be scared and pious together) that filled my soul with contentment. If they were less charged than similarly fulfilling times with women, that was part of their appeal. I have had an increasing, deepening experience of the fact that my wife and I are best friends to one another, and from this I have derived some central theses about the theology of marriage. It remains for me to take these matters up with Jesus, however, and until I do, my spirituality for men probably will not be worth very much.

With my best friends, strength and vulnerability change sides. We are open to one another, now more, now less, in good times and bad, in sickness and in health. The classical phrase was that a friend is *dimidium animae meae*: half of my soul. Can men apply that to Jesus? Are men in fact applying that to Jesus all the time, with me simply out of touch, marginal because of my secularism and sin? I do not know the way to answer the second question, except to say that most of the men I meet in a typical month tell me nothing about their prayer, indeed rarely give signs of praying. But surely the answer to the first question is yes, men can apply the classical sense of friendship to Jesus, the sense of sharing one another's souls, of having a likeness of mind that makes communication almost instantaneous, of always being able to rely on one another's concern and loyalty.

Is there something in U.S. culture or the American male subcultures (varied somewhat along ethnic lines), that inhibits sharing at deep levels, soul to soul? The answer clearly seems yes. And yet when one tries to specify this inhibiting something, only a general social bias against men's displaying emotion or revealing their inmost thoughts (which also means inmost feelings) steps forward. Our sexual stereotyping has made emotion and revelation women's affairs, and other cultures have polarized the sexes similarly. Yet we know, when we are honest and wise, that thought and emotion cohere at the center of every person, strongly allied in the measure that the person is creative, intense, engaged, alive. The more human a man, the more a *Mensch*, the more he is understanding as well as strong, sympathetic as well as resolute.

But to advance deep sharing between men, including sharing with Jesus, we will have to include the vulnerable flank of men's emotions. It is not enough to show understanding and sympathy. We will have to include fear, doubt, hurt, confusion. Today, it takes great courage for a man to admit to any such vulnerability or negativity. He is bound to expect that such an admission will seem weak, womanly, wimpy. The price exacted by our continuing to treat men as though they should be warriors is their burying their fears, even from themselves. True, some men have wives, sisters, or female friends to whom they can speak out their worries. By the canons we have established, men are allowed now and then to show such women their raw, tender sides. But only rarely do our men share the pathos of their mortality and darkness, let alone cry together. I am no exception to this rule. Most days, I meet disappointments, reasons for fear, even the death of family members and friends like a good Stoic. I do know, from studying prayer, the value of opening my heart to God, and I have, on occasion, simply let go. But only rarely have I done this explicitly with Jesus, and the main reason probably is that whereas it is relatively easy to make disclosures to a sufficiently vast, vague, and all-knowing "God, " "Jesus" calls to mind another man, and I don't want another man to see me as lacking self-control or toughness.

For another day, one might reflect on the love of the Logos, but it is clear that for this day getting some purchase on the love of Jesus will be accomplishment enough. To consider Jesus my friend in the non-syrupy but fully affectionate way for which I am groping, I might of course pay more attention to his vulnerability. Christ on the cross not only died for my sins, as the old manuals constantly repeated, he suffered shamefully, most exposedly, as a criminal, a figure of contempt. The gospels certainly show him retaining his dignity, and their theologies insist that he kept control. But the humanity in him touches the humanity in me most deeply when I realize the risks he took, the power of the shame that must have gripped him. He had lost, been rejected, been accounted a fool.

If I get a migraine headache, I feel ashamed. To lose my speech, to be wounded and dysfunctional, to cause bystanders to give me the look they give the crippled or the retarded, cause me to blush and withdraw. I want to be alone to lick my wounds, which are more psychic than physical. I need help to laugh at this passing debility and be reminded that things soon will be normal again. What can I do for Jesus in his shame? Putting aside all the distinctions and guidelines orthodox Christology might prompt, how can I go to him and be compassionate, really enter into what he was willing to do and be "for us men and our salvation," as the old translations of the creedal phrase put it?

Would Jesus countenance my taking him in my arms, my not prefacing every sentence with "Lord," my telling him how much I admire his courage, my confessing that I could never have done it, my more relevantly confessing I do not do even the sliver of it I might do if I believed he wanted to give himself in me and my circumstances today? Would he want gratitude, sorrow, succor? Obviously he would, if our faith is correct in insisting upon his full humanity, like us in all things save sin. Probably the women who stayed faithful at the cross while the men fled understood this. And so, probably what keeps men like me from doing it is a debility women might help us reduce.

⧬ 3 ⧬

The Father

IN THE NEXT CHAPTER I SHALL DEAL
with a love of the Holy Spirit that might bear sexual overtones,
and with the perichoresis, the mutual indwelling, of the three divine persons. Here I want to continue the focus, the structure,
implied when we take Jesus as the bringer of eschatological salvation.

As is well known, Jesus' use of "Abba" for God was distinc-
tive. Scholars rummaging through the contemporary rabbinic
literature may debate precisely how distinctive it was, but even
if they narrow the novelty of Jesus' usage, we do well to take it
seriously. Of the many books on Jesus I have read, Lucas Grollenberg's modest work still seems to me to have come closest to
the likely heart of the matter.[6] Grollenberg stresses the singular

trust that Jesus reposed in his Father. From that trust, Jesus was able to move through life much more freely than the rest of us. He did not need the defenses that keep us from appreciating, understanding, enjoying, and helping out one another as we might. He did not fear the political establishment of his time nor avert his face from the divine mystery. Thinking, experiencing that the Father was always with him, on his side, for him, Jesus showed us what human nature might be, were we to let love bring our potential to maturity. The world was his oyster, because all good things descended to him from his Father of lights.

Two brief scenarios may suggest my own stumbling efforts to enter into this filial relationship to God, and so may illumine some of the considerations germane to a better spirituality for men. The first is rather negative. I have observed, in several settings, a marriage of theological suspicion of human nature and academic critical-mindedness that has thrown up huge obstacles to a love of God on the model of Jesus' filial trust. The theological suspicion, in fact, has come from Calvinist tenets, but one could easily write the same scenario from Catholic Jansenist sources. Quite explicitly, colleagues have shown that they have taken to heart the doctrine of human corruption tendered them by their masters, and the result has been a practical, political program with the motto, "We'd better get those bastards before they get us." More subtly, but ultimately more corrosively, this theology has made the colleagues I have in mind constantly second-guess, if not indeed hate, themselves. There, the motto has been: "Because I too am a corrupt bastard, I'd better rein in my natural instincts and favor the opposite of what I'd like."

When one couples this theology with the negatively critical mind sharpened by higher education—the ability to poke holes and debunk, which most graduate programs foster much better than they foster the ability to create and complement—the result usually is outright debacle. No exchange is straightforward. Most prejudgments are unfavorable. The hermeneutic of suspicion moves from the role of adjutant, where it is quite helpful, to the role of king, where it rides roughshod over the fragile bonds one needs to build collaborative enterprises, works of art, friendships, and people who pray to a Father they believe delights in them.

The second scenario, quite positive, comes from Ash Wednesday of a past Lent in our chapel in Tulsa. With a nice ecumenical touch, the choirmaster had prepared a Mozart Kyrie and Credo, which our kids in robes and sneakers sang like cherubim. I was amazed how quickly the tears came to my eyes and how long it took to swallow down the lump in my throat. Beauty ever ancient, ever new—how long since I had heard such praise of God? I thought of European cathedrals we have visited and the sense of tradition, continuity, and solace handed down for centuries that they conjure up. I thought of Karl Rahner forgiving the church all its heartlessness and abuse, because it still has been a place where one could hear the words of eternal life, where one could receive the sacraments of immortality. Loving the almighty father, the maker of heaven and earth, of all things visible and invisible, that the Mozart credo was praising, I felt my cynicism melt away. Suddenly, it was minimalist expectations and stoic endurance that were on the defensive. Suddenly, the largess of God was obvious, and the burden of proof was on our human pusillanimity. And, with this came a Pauline anamnesis: If God is for us and has given us the Son, how can God fail to give us all things with him? Nothing can separate us from the love of God in Christ Jesus our Lord.

One of the several emphases of Rahnerian Christology that helped to usher in a new phase of reflection on the meaning of Jesus was the insistence that we take seriously the fact that only the Logos, the Son, took flesh. On one level, this is stuff from the Baltimore Catechism. On another level, however, our failure to appropriate it in popular theology has contributed to our preaching and praying as though the community of divine persons did not exist. Practically speaking, few Western Christians are trinitarians, aware that their exchanges of knowing and lov-

ing flow into and out from the processions of the divine knowing and loving. Few Western Christians have appropriated with
conceptual clarity the consequences of their being incorporated
into the incarnate Logos, and so oriented toward the Father and
the Spirit as Jesus was. Begotten from unbegotten, light from
light—these primordial symbols mean little to most men I
know, even those who pray. My own prayer is more apophatic
than defined, but I love the drift of such symbols into the divine
immensity, the fathomless memory that Augustine associated
with the Father. The Abba of Jesus is the generativity of all creation, the explosive force of the stars, the strong bonds of the at-
oms, the light of the Logos who shines in every human insight.
Yet Jesus, like Elijah, seems regularly to have experienced him
as a small, still voice, as one so powerful he could be utterly gentle.

Primordial symbols such as these intertwine with our deepest
psychic formation, making our relations with our parents what
one might call our natal theological endowment. My father has
been dead more than fifteen years; yet, as soon as I start to ponder trinitarian love, he is with me as though I were back in high
school. It amazes me that my memories of him grow more and
more compassionate. Apart from shedding a few tears at beauty like that of a Mozart Kyrie, I seldom cry. The last time I wept
full out was at my father's wake, when the definitive proof of
his vulnerability lay before me. I do not want to trade on his al-
coholism, his struggles to run a small business, his wasting by
cancer, but I do want to understand the poignancy they still carry. The more he has moved away from my childish expectations of fatherhood, where I naturally looked for strength and
stability, the more patripassianism has seemed to me orthodox.

I do not mean, of course, that I want to contend literally for
the position that God the Father suffered on the cross. I mean
that the risk of God, the vulnerability of God, the engagement of
God the source in all the pathos of his creatures, have slowly
started to dawn. How one squares this with the perfection of

God, in which I also believe, can remain a question for another day. Here, I am interested in the love summoned when one joins the complete trustworthiness of God that Jesus depended on with the risks of parenthood that any of our human fathers or mothers has experienced. What could be more ordinary than sexual attraction, conception, and birth—and what more extraordinary in creatures who now and then realize what they are getting into?

Our Father, who is in heaven, presumably knew exactly what he was getting into. Though creation as a work *ad extra* traditionally has been attributed to God as one, I find it especially fitting to make the Lord's Prayer thanks for the decision of the unbegotten source to communicate the divine substance, beyond the perfect, defectless sharing he has always had with the Son and the Spirit, to us very defective creatures. When God not only makes us and saves us but divinizes us, takes us into the bosom of the trinitarian relations, our mortal flesh should move on to keeping silence, which often is our purest praise. The fatherhood of God, like the messiahship of Christ and the down payment on our immortality vouchsafed in the Spirit, is not too strange to be believed but too good. Few things would do more to revitalize the spirituality of Christian men than for us to take to heart the trinitarian symbols of what God has given us, of the way God always wants to be for us an Abba more intimate than we are to ourselves.

⚘ 4 ⚘

The Spirit

JUST AS OUR CONCEPTION OF THE
fatherhood of God is shaped by Christ's usage, so is our conception of the Holy Spirit. Jesus seems to have prayed to God the
Father and experienced the guidance of God the Spirit.[7] And, I
have already referred to the role of comforter assigned the Spirit
by the Johannine Christ. But average Catholic spirituality probably has done less to develop the riches of the symbolism of the
Spirit than it has done with the Father. For weal or woe, our
love of the Father is bound up with our experience of human pa-
ternity. What experiences ought to give our love of the Spirit focus and resonance?

Certainly, we can explore the analogies to teaching, guiding,
and comforting that Scripture suggests. Certainly wisdom, pro-

phetic inspiration, brooding, and nursing also come to mind.
The Johannine Spirit is "another" paraclete, which suggests that
Jesus was the first and that the Spirit is carrying on invisibly
what Jesus labored at visibly. I think any of these notions, perhaps especially those associated with wisdom, holds out rich
promise. Whenever I have pondered the new, interior covenant
foreseen by Jeremiah, I have hoped that the Spirit might be fill-
ing many hearts with ingiven, connatural knowledge. Whenever I have savored the Sequence for Pentecost, with its images of
watering what is arid, washing what is dirtied, I have felt greatly comforted.

As many of these images suggest, the Spirit can bear us a feminine persona. God alone knows the way we may best handle
the complications thrust upon us by today's awareness of sexist
overtones in our traditional language for worship and our traditional theological conceptions, but perhaps letting this feminine
persona of the Spirit emerge into explicit consciousness would
help.

The reasons the church fathers shied away from sexual analogies for the trinitarian persons no doubt were valid in their day,
when the Hellenistic mysteries often had orgiastic overtones or
dealt with fertility more materially than Christian instinct de-
sired. In our day, however, divine fatherhood without divine
motherhood can seem to warp our theology, and so our entire
religious life. We may still want to avoid androgyny on the
model of, for example, Hindu theology, but we should take a
lesson from Jewish Wisdom, Buddhist Wisdom (Prajnaparami-
ta), and Chinese reflection on the Tao, all of which carry feminine overtones. If we men were to begin to let the Spirit mother
us, parallel to the way we should let the first trinitarian person
father us, we might open a door to psycho-symbolic energies we
have kept shut to our detriment. The same would apply to
women, all the more so in a time when feminists have been
probing the ambiguities of mother-daughter relations.

What are these psychosomatic energies men have tended to

keep shut or leave untapped? Some probably go back to earliest childhood, when a maternal countenance, a Madonna, represented comfort, nourishment, most of the world. Others stem from the time when we had to cut some of the ties to our mothers in order to fit into male roles. The psychoanalytic overtones to these references can complicate men's using them, either personally or theologically, but with practice and perseverance we might find them less threatening. Then "mothering" could connote not simply the always open arms and heart we associate with maternity (I bracket the very relevant question of how one handles less than ideal experiences of motherhood, and the associated question of how men are to get realistic expectations of fallible, fully human women), but also the coach, the buddy, the teacher, the nurse—all the other roles that healthy mothers play, making use of an ease or familiarity our culture tends to deny fathers.

In our culture women are allowed a closeness to children, a diminishing of the distances that age and authority might create, that most men have to work to seize. If we could think of the Holy Spirit as close, playful, supportive, wise in the ways that the best moms are when they guide their kids through the shoals of childhood and adolescence, we might offer men helps to relax with God, unbutton their stuffed shirts, laugh and cry with the mystery that bore them and knows their every quirk. The solemnity attaching to so much traditional spirituality (largely fashioned by and for men), the assumption that one is going into the presence of the king and ought to be quite proper, could be diluted, and with it much constriction. If we cannot be at home with our God, cannot feel known and at ease the way we are with the women we love and trust, laughing and groaning as the circumstances suggest, we cannot be fair to God's whole mystery and goodness, which certainly must contain every kind of love and supple kindness we stereotypically associate with mothers and sisters, female lovers and friends. And of course we, not God, will be the losers, because we will not feel the consolations the Spirit is eager to extend to us.

My own mother is still living, and I have more work to do on my relation with her before I shall feel comfortable in publicizing implications for the love of God parallel to those I noted in my relations with my father. I can say, though, that a motif of deepening compassion for what she has suffered in her imperfect life and growing admiration for her courage suggests more likeness to what I have thought about divine fatherhood than difference.

The major hat I wear is that of a writer, so sometimes I have experienced the Holy Spirit as a muse, a creative lover. Writing is a strange occupation, though perhaps no stranger than teaching, counseling, and other occupations greatly shaped by biorhythms and grooves one cannot control. If my experience is representative, those who write regularly never know precisely what they are going to come out with. We have our notes, our outlines, our heuristic suspicions, but what appears on the paper or word processor screen is always something of a surprise. Thus, it is commonplace for novelists to speak of having a character lead them into situations they had not anticipated. It is common to hear theologians speak of unexpected twists and turns in the data, but less common to hear them speak of shifts wrought through their exposition of the data. That may suggest that most theologians are more scholars than writers: people more focused on their data than on summoning the phantasms in which insights into their data might be multiplied.

At any rate, writers like me are married to their muse. The conversation with the self that gets externalized on the screen of the word processor involves more than the self, and sometimes quite obviously so. Probably the typical writer thinks that this more is the unconscious, the murky depths from which the most important glimmers and hunches pop up. However, there is no reason for the Christian writer, or the Christian worker in any other field that regularly depends on a modest inspiration, not to conceive of this process as an intercourse with the Holy Spirit.

Many of the suggestions that come from one's depths carry marks of gratuity. Not all of them prove workable, of course—writers, too, must discern the spirits—but many of them imply that what is going on in one's depths includes a fairly regular reminding by a greater Spirit. If you can smile and abide it, you can use the simile of your mother's call not to forget your lunch (where you get your nourishment), or her rougher taking you by the shoulders and spinning you ninety degrees, so that you finally see the monkeys you were missing.

Intercourse with the Spirit conjures up other possibilities, of course, and I want to use the rest of this chapter to ponder them. Others thinking about a spirituality for men may have explored erotic love of the Spirit, but I have not seen much in this line. Usually, the discussion of spiritual marriage takes God as the bridegroom and treats the soul as the bride. From the Song of Songs to John of the Cross and Teresa of Avila, this has been a very profitable venture. But I want to pursue the possibility of men extending their eros for women into spiritual depths where we would be romancing our God. If it is legitimate for women or the feminized soul to be both child of God and spouse, it should be legitimate for the masculine portion of our psyches to be both child of the maternal Spirit and lover of the divine beauty, fertility, subtlety, wisdom—all of the faces of God that by cultural tradition shine with a feminine smile.

Even in my acedia and secularity, I find days when I am ravenous for God. Sometimes it is the beauty of the day, with the sun dancing off the river. Recently it was a delightful afternoon at the zoo, when two polar bears entertained us for an hour with their antics in the pool: wrestling, cannonballing, trying a little backstroke, hauling themselves out like the nimble Mark Spitz who never doubted he would win in a breeze.

The play of nature in the spring, the release of all that sap, must have figured in the Aristotelian understanding of the good: that which all things desire. In the spring all of nature desires fertility, increase, prospering that we humans associate with intimate love. In the spring, the longing for God, the consummate beauty, seems but a gracious gilding of what all God's creatures are feeling. But there are summer, fall, and winter variations on such eros. There is the love associated with the death of the days at the winter solstice, with the death of one's creativity in blockages, with the disappointment inevitably experienced with both fallible human beings and one's perhaps more fallible self. From depression and disgust can rise the most ardent longing: Get me out of this, help me find comfort, solace, and fulfillment in a transcendent embrace.

In pouring ourselves into the Spirit, being taken to her bosom, perhaps we experience something of the divine mutuality and suffusion. In the Spirit, the Father and the Son have their unity, their merely relational distinction. The Spirit who is their breath of love is also, in patristic usage, the kiss uniting them. Without the perfection and purity of the divine perichoresis, but still most usefully, we might play with the lovely Spirit, giving and receiving, praising and admiring. And such a spiritual experiment might do wonders for our peculiarly, though of course not uniquely Catholic, unease with sexuality. If a fully passionate intercourse with the Spirit became legitimate, many of our questions about the theology of marriage and the single state, and many of our ethical dilemmas about contraception, artificial insemination, and even abortion might arrange themselves in new, less fearful patterns.

Part Two

The Love of Self

ᗡ 5 ᗡ

The Self as Embodied

IF I WERE MORE CLEARLY INVOLVED in a romance with the Holy Spirit than has been the leitmotiv of my spiritual life to date, I also might do a better job at overcoming the dualism that seems to afflict all human beings, but perhaps especially men. This dualism appears in the masculine struggle to keep sexual appetite and love together and maintain an integral image of women. It appears in the many contemporary cultural movements to repristinate good health and emotional satisfaction, giving brother ass his due. Certainly, the struggles required to achieve wholeness are a major sign of our aboriginal division. Certainly, the Catholic convictions about sacramentality and grace's building on nature should be sufficient protection against the neo-paganism wafting in many discussions of diet, exercise, and emotional satisfaction.

At age thirty, I found myself in sunny California, looking for exercise. I went to the gym at Stanford and discovered that on the West Coast standing 5' 10" high meant never touching the basketball. Every kid seemed at least 6' 3".

So I bought Kenneth Cooper's book on aerobics and left the world of competition for the world of fitness, sure I was responding to a saintly daimon. Of course, immediately I began competing with myself, trying to get my time for the mile under seven minutes. And, whenever I could, I roared past some plausible equal on the homestretch, to the cheers of the Olympic crowd. But it was fun, it did push away the tensions of graduate school, and it brought back thoughts about my body that had first hatched when I was a "midget" swimmer.

As a ten year old, I was a great backstroker—the best in the circuit of New England Boys' Clubs at the awesome distance of twenty-five yards. As a twelve year old, I was into what was then considered serious training: a mile a day. And I did it willingly, somehow realizing that it was good for all of me, mind as well as body. When Cooper later gave me the concept, I realized that twenty years previously I had experienced the "training effect" prized by knights of the grail of cardiovascular health. At the time, I had known only that when my second wind came, I would feel I could go on forever. Seventy-two laps made a mile, but one hundred were not beyond me.

I now swim and push the staves of a NordicTrack, still seeking the grail and enjoying the training effect. The swimming is like a return to the sea from which all of our genes came, a somatic homecoming. The skiing is a salutary exercise in working and working and going nowhere, perhaps like Gandhi's spinning wheel. For Gandhi, the spinning wheel symbolized karmayoga, the work done for its own sake, without desire. For me, each session on the NordicTrack now says things about aging and moderation, things the midget swimmer did not have to deal with. I have good days, usually correlated with winter cold

and high pressure skies, when the temptation is to do too much.
I have more draggy days, when the Tulsa heat and humidity call
for another sort of caution. Slowly, I am accepting that my tendency is to do too much rather than too little. Slowly, I am acknowledging the stitch in the side or the flutter in the chest that
once I would have paid no mind. The body is such a marvel. It
both does and does not have predictable patterns. Almost always I begin in heaviness, finding the exercise difficult and dis-
couraging. At about 10-15 minutes the sweat starts to come, and
my body says, "I like it." Anything beyond a half hour calls for
conferences between body and mind, tricks to keep the legs
pumping, reasons not to keep upping the goal. All of this is predictable, and yet now and then I am sure I should go for a full
hour. As well, now and then I cannot make twenty minutes, or
the fine feeling that came from a brisk thirty-five minutes falls
apart into a migraine. The fragile vessels in which we carry the
life of God are not ours to command like computers. They are
more like obedient servants who occasionally let us know they
are fed up.

I imagine one could write similar reflections about patterns of
hunger and satiety, patterns of sleep, patterns of sexual love,
menstrual patterns, ups and downs in one's practice of medi-
cine, teaching, or other works. In all of them the message I
would expect is that our action is also a passion, our cooperation
with the Holy Spirit is really a junior partnership.

As some readers perhaps noted, most of my suggestions for
men's love of God suggested a more active role than traditional
spirituality tended to propose. Especially with the Holy Spirit,
but also with the Father and Christ, I found myself thinking
thoughts of erotic initiative or compassionate appreciation that
come from what might stereotypically be called men's strength.
It is not that I want to deny men's weakness, nor the blessedness
of feeling small yet safe in the house of God. It is just that when
I tried to think of the ways of loving God that might engage me
more than what I had been taught and now tend to do, these

more active, perhaps more mature possibilities emerged. But for this present matter of loving one's embodied self, the message coming to me from exercise and people-watching calls for greater moderation, seconding, and responsiveness. It sends me images of rejecting the workaholism I find rampant, the excess in many men's range of commitments. I want to take more time for prayer, thought, reading, leisure, romantic conversation, making love. I want to see more of God's beautiful world and show more flexibility in responding to cries for help. Maybe this, too, is a reflection of my trying to come to grips with middle age. I seemed to have crossed a threshold, so that now often I no longer should, can, or fully want to swim an extra half mile or jam in another writing commitment.

I associate our so frequent overwork with the problem of loving the embodied self because usually the toll being taken shows itself in the ache in my neck and the irritability in my voice. By the time summer comes and we get to the beach, I have narrowed my range of perception, appreciation, and pleasure to perhaps half of what it will be after the waves have worked their therapy. I am still not sure what the optimal balance is between the drive that gets things done and brings one to that peculiar fatigue that is highly creative, and the drive that clearly is abusive and detrimental. Women, of course, have their drives, and perhaps more importantly the myriad ways they are put upon, but the paradigm of type A behavior I have in mind seems indebted to testosterone. With no wild boars and tigers to slay, no Visigoths to beat back, we men regularly displace our aggression onto our work, competing with nature, other workers, and ourselves for both the joy of it and the hell. Not only do we die younger than women, we take a longer time to gain subtlety, wholeness, and what the Taoists call *wu-wei*: creative inaction, not-doing that makes everything run better. Good government, Lao Tzu says, is like cooking fish: the less stirring the better. Intrusive testosterone does not learn this easily. Receptive estrogen has a lot to teach it during those long winter nights when the hormones get to bundling.

So, to love the self God has given us, we middle-aged men probably need to think thoughts of letting go, praying for better perspective, trusting God to show us new, even better possibilities in ceding responsibilities, accepting retirements, appreciating the chant of ecological science that most intrusion is more complicated, and more deleterious, than we initially suspect. We need to convince ourselves that overwork is a vice—an ugly sin. We need to ask God for help in acting upon this conviction, when that will take us against the drift of our fellow-workers. And we need, finally, to think well of our bodies for finally forcing us to these realizations. If we were wise, we would long ago have budgeted more time for our wives, children, and friends. Better late than never, though. As Rabbi Hillel said, If not now, when?

6

The Self as Spirit

RABBI HILLEL, LIKE ALL RELIGIOUS masters, was especially interested in having people move their minds and hearts to the love of God. No doubt he wanted us to be kind to our bodies, but he realized that we come from dust and unto dust we all return. It is the spark in our clod, as Lonergan once put it, that rightly is judged more imperative. Only when we love the One God with whole minds, hearts, souls, and strengths will our bodies be fully sacramental.

Extending the theme of mercy rather than sacrifice that I found exercise urging when it came to loving the self as embodied, let us now think kindly thoughts about our spirits, especially about the way the spirits of men usually have been formed to think, love, and pray. A book such as the insightful *Women's*

Ways of Knowing reminds us that the academic establishment still thinks of men's knowing as detached, impersonal, and objective.[8] When it combines this assumption with an imposition of such a model on all students, women as much as men, it doubles the damages.

Religious men and women may be somewhat comforted to note that the models of knowing suggested by prayer and community life dispute the academic stereotype. Any writers on prayer worth their salt soon come to contemplation, just as any epistemologists worth their salt soon deal with a judgment much deeper and more holistic than understanding. For a Michael Polanyi, our knowledge is more tacit than express, and in any venture it is wholly personal. For an Eric Voegelin, the only epistemologist who can appreciate the noetic breakthrough achieved by Plato and Aristotle is one who can sense the way God is the mover of our desire to know. *The Cloud of Unknowing* is perhaps the most apposite classic on the ways that interpersonal knowledge of God greatly relativizes what one can achieve by ratiocination. The advice of Einstein that one should attend to what scientists do in their creative work, rather than to the paradigms of scientific method they pontifically enounce, suggests that the regnant academic models no more respond to first rate science than they do to creative work in the humanities or the knowledge God gives in prayer.

The knowledge God gives in prayer, I suspect, is a knowledge well called faith, and well described as born of religious love. It is good to understand what one can of the creeds and the mainstream theologians, but God becomes a rock and salvation exorcizing our worst fears only when God has touched us heart to heart. We have to commune with God to know God, and unless we know God, we do not know the most important things about ourselves, other people, or the natural world. We have to speak to God, listen to God, and endure God's silences. Sometimes we will feel like a motherless child, adrift in an uncaring world. Sometimes we will feel like idiots, people so singular they neither understand others nor can be understood. These are the times when it is hard to love our spiritual selves, to think well of God's handiwork.

But perhaps the hardest times come when we have run from God, hiding like our first parents. If we are honest, we know we have no excuse, not the thinnest fig-leaf to cover us. Adapting Augustine, we instinctively think, "It was foul, and I loved it." Imitating Judas, we exit into a night of further betrayal and despair, thinking even God can do little for us. Then, the love of ourselves has to hope that the Spirit will remind us that nothing can separate us, that God is always greater than our hearts. Then, we have to realize, in all humiliation, that we were but rookies, spouting the right words about sinfulness but not appreciating their omni-relevance. Let nothing disturb us, not even our sin? I want to believe it could be so. I want to think that love of self rests on the love of God that shines on just and unjust alike. If we ask God for the bread that is forgiveness as well as immortality, will God give us a stone? Is it possible to overstate the goodness of God, or our own foolishness in thinking we can block out the sun? No doubt we must not sin to magnify God's power of forgiveness, but when we do sin, must we not let that sin itself induce God to be Father, Brother, Lover?

The man who has an addiction, a dirty secret, the remorse of having been cold to his children, or just the fatigue of feeling himself a religious mediocrity probably finds it harder to bear these burdens than he might because his culture has warped his sense of self as much as it has warped his sense of the way he knows. When I worked briefly at the Boston City Hospital, or when I listened to friends who worked with the poor, I came to admire those who let themselves become familiar enough with grime, failure, and even betrayal to see them with clear eyes, even to feel them with forgiving hearts.

Recently, I took a walk to a convenience store nearby to get some air, some oatmeal, and a newspaper. On the way home, I saw a trio of Indians on the steps of a sagging house marked "Bailbondsman." The two men were in jackets appropriate to the forty degree weather. The woman, sitting on the steps, wore only a thin, short-sleeved blouse, and she was crying. I wondered why she was crying, but so many possibilities came to mind that thinking about that seemed futile. So, I seized on the reason she had no jacket, and the reason one of the men didn't give her his. I was well past before I thought of giving her mine, and I was somehow aware that the men would take offense. But the woman is still there in my mind, cold and crying.

Ah, Lord, what do we do with all the cold and crying of the world's five billions? What does that do to their bodies, their spirits, the spirits of us spectators? I feel guilty not only for my own sins but for my place in the system of sin summoned to mind by an abused Indian woman. Comfortable and metaphysical, I probe the compassion that might ease the fallenness of history, realizing as I do that I have virtually given up on economics and politics. Voegelin took as one of his touchstones what the most idealistic people make of the politics of their era. Weaned on Socrates and Plato, forced to run for his life from Nazi Austria, he was not optimistic. What does it do to the spirit of good men when their impulse to take charge and set things right comes back at them like a boomerang stamped "useless"? What does it do to the spirit of any of us when our church wants no dissent and insists that the female half of us cannot represent Christ at the sacraments?

We need gentle spiritual succor, offered to those most burdened by such evils, and offered by ourselves to ourselves. We need the Spirit's help in spreading on the wounds a balm that might keep depression from becoming despair. Nothing can separate us from God, not even the church of God, which of course we are. As long as God is God, any idealistic generation may marshal the critical mass and start an exodus out of slavery and back to the foundations of genuine patriotism and pride in the church. The problem is not that the spiritual masters have left us no wisdom about right order. The problem is that we, the mass of us human beings, do not know this wisdom and will not use it. Money, honors, and pride—what spiritual tradition has not estimated their dangers like an architect imagining every possible stress and strain? If we cannot achieve the full therapy of moving our culture to re-embody right order, we can at least succor our spirits in meditative reading and prayer.

For my own spirit, I am moving toward a redefinition of my work, with hopes that when I reach fifty I shall have fulfilled the obligations incurred through years of trying to earn a living and finally be able to labor at a new sort of theology, a reflection interested in the traces of right order that God has left everywhere. The content is not as important at this present juncture as the therapeutic goal. I want to work at what offers the best prospects for healing and strengthening people's spirits. I want to pay back to the Rahners and Lonergans, the Voegelins and Polanyis, the pittance that a grateful disciple can. And, I want to do this with explicitly contemporary Catholic faith, occupying the hardly demilitarized zone between Roman theology and the riches of all the religious treasuries God has inspired. It is a quixotic task, but I love to contemplate it. In contemplating it, I find I am loving my spiritual self, because I am finding grounds for hoping that soon I may be able more leisurely, more avowedly, to study the ways of God, especially those as far from our our destructive ways as the heavens are from the earth, and to help publicize the freedom they offer.

Part Three

The Love of Neighbor

∽ 7 ∾

Women

THE CHRISTIAN GOLDEN RULE
presumably very important to any Christian spirituality, is that
we should love our neighbors as ourselves. In the present section, let us reflect on what this might mean for the love today's
men show women.

My first impulse is to say that a spirituality for men would be
innovative and helpful if it merely brought us to show women
considerably more warmth, understanding, and playfulness.
One of the important strands in the malaise between the sexes is
our legacy of mistrust. This legacy, in turn, owes much to the
spiritual writers who depicted women as the main dangers to
men's religious fidelity. Other factors certainly pitched in, but
the contribution of Christian tradition to the souring of what
ought to be mutual delight between men and women is a sorry

chapter. Our fathers have eaten sour grapes, so all of us today have our teeth set on edge about sexuality. In the popular mind, sex is the Catholic neurosis, and the popular mind is quite right.

Play comes to mind as a key criterion of how things are going between men and women, because romance, friendship, and marriage all only round out to their best potential when the partners help one another play, expose new sides of themselves, energize their imaginations, and stand against the crippling seriousness that can afflict the worlds of work, church life, and education. People only play well when they are relaxed, feel at home, and are buoyed by trust and love. Thus, there should be much play and laughter in the house of God, the Body of Christ, since that should be Christians' happy home. There should be teasing, flirting, challenging, picking up and twirling around between Christian men and women. Such play, I believe, not only bars the door against many idolatries and self-importances, it also loosens the bow so that when hard times come we can have the give and the resilience necessary to handle them well.

It is commonplace to note that much of what passes for play in men's circles is highly competitive. From golf to poker, many men's behavior at supposed play is as stressed, as driven, as when they are buying, selling, banking, and producing scholarship. Thus the light mind and light touch that bring release from such drivenness become significant gifts. Some men possess them and share them, of course, but stereotypically our culture considers such gifts more feminine than masculine. Where "he" is grave and weighty, "she" can be humorous, good at caricature and debunking. Nowadays women are playful at their peril, risking not only traditional male dismissal as superficial but also scorn from many in the sisterhood, who seem to think rigor, haughtiness, and aggression essential to a serious portfolio. Thus both sexes continue to be warped by stereotypes, and play suffers all around, diminishing the delight God has coded in our hormones.

I think the Spirit of God smiles ruefully at such warping,

again wishing that her charges would settle down and seize their freedom. Wanting to make us free spirits, the Spirit must be behind those little inspirations that occasionally move Doctor Samuel to shut off his beeper and Professor Samantha to let down her hair. For in the aftermath of our inspired moments of play, we tend to be humbler and more realistic. The fact is that we are all dancing on thin ice over perilous depths of meaninglessness and disaster. Christian faith cannot be tragic—the resurrection of Christ forbids it. Even when our hearts condemn us, God is greater than our hearts. Even when legions of doubters continue to make God an angry sovereign, the Father of Jesus goes out to meet his prodigal children. Whether we can play, tease, and find our attractions and beguilements cause for praising God says a great deal about our faith. I was reminded of this recently when a dying friend, three days before entering his final coma, teased me about the tie I was wearing and joshed that his brother's kindly ministrations were quite out of character. For a moment his playfulness beat back his cancer. For a moment, I knew he had already cast himself out into God's mystery.

Over the years I have dealt with a number of women suffering through bad marriages. I have been amazed at how much they have accepted from blocked, stupid, hurtful husbands. They have had their own failings, of course, but again and again their disorder and sickness have seemed a mirror of their husbands'. One of the most poignant things I have witnessed has been the loss of confidence that even gifted, beautiful women have suffered. They have been so grateful for a little admiration and affection that I have learned to offer these quite carefully.

I do not think this means that men should reenforce their stereotypical image of strength, silence, and having no needs. I do think it means that listening, showing affection, and being playful are no mean virtues. With spouses, friends, and little girls, men have an opportunity to make themselves, the primordial other in women's experience and the most basic stranger, seem trustworthy rather than threatening. Certainly, women are not automatically bonded to other women and certainly, one of the rightful goals of feminism is to help women overcome the cultural trends that would make them distrust other women. But it remains that men are somatic strangers as fellow women are not, and this is only intensified when most men are physically stronger and culturally more prized. More times than not, women are dealing with men who possess more power—physical, financial, institutional—than they do. More times than not, men first honor the Christian golden rule by being aware of this and trying to undercut it. When men communicate that they think of women as their intellectual equals, when they suggest that they value women's experience as much as men's and have at least a glimmer about women's problems, they contribute a reconciliation, an atonement, at least as foundational as that redressing economic or racial grievances.

From this initial stress on showing appreciation and affection, men then have to move to the other side of equality, which implies receiving as well as giving. Receiving is at least as complicated as giving. Sacramentally, for example, men have been willing to minister to women, but to date our male-dominated church is not willing to sanction a full ministry of women to men. Of course, all sorts of ministries go on both formally and informally, but many more are aborted because male power-holders cannot see themselves receiving the eucharistic Christ from women. Giving and receiving ideally balance, so a spirituality for equals implies an even flow. Part of the flow is the gifts the two genders have evolved throughout history, and part is peculiar to the given exchange. So women stereotypically offer receptivity and fertility, while men offer initiative and protection. Yet, Mary A is quicker off the mark than her husband John Z, so in their household she initiates the financial planning, the moves to new jobs, the sex, while he provides the second thoughts, the seconding affirmations, the late night "What a good idea!"

Their love of women should make men think of the biblical "flesh of my flesh and bone of my bone," without the patriarchalism of Adam's rib. It should be the main delight in most men's lives, extended when the women they love are reflected in their children. I do not think fathers should spoil their daughters, but I can understand the reason they do. Here is a miniature of the bounce and vulnerability that first seized their hearts; so, even when it is bratty, they may tend to indulge it. And, as long as our cultures ask women to represent beauty more than they ask this of men, fathers will have a special obligation to help their daughters feel they are beautiful. To be sure, this should go along with helping them feel they are bright and capable. It should not encourage manipulation or the daughters' becoming clinging vines. But it should let them think that snuggling in a man's embrace is part of their blessed birthright. It should give them a foundational confidence that they can give their beauty, their fertility, their competence, their love because it will all be cherished and returned.

I have the feeling that what I have said thus far risks sentimentality, but I do not want to qualify it any further. Often my wife's observations have led me to think that many women who are in pain actually ask very little—which, of course, only doubles the poignancy of their situations. I am not thinking of the statistics that show how many more of the burdens of poverty fall on women, and the children for whom women have the primary care, than fall on men, though these statistics are a fine antidote to sentimentality. I am thinking of the nun who works as a campus minister for $9,000 a year and cannot even get her bishop to answer her letters. I am thinking of the divorced woman who cannot get her ex-husband to visit their sons. I am thinking of the woman whose husband rarely makes love to her, largely because he stays up so late each night working and drinking. And, I am thinking of the myriad women, the great groaning chorus, who complain that their men will not talk to them, are unwilling to share.

Sometimes women do not understand the pressures on men, and sometimes they do not understand a healthy male taciturnity; but, on the whole, I find women usually willing to go 60 percent of the way. It is possible that the Indian woman who was sitting on the porch of the bailbondsman was the main culprit in that scene of domestic tragedy, but the odds seem against it. Women certainly have to work on their sins of weakness, but I sympathize with the complexity such work must carry. If they are to preserve the receptivity, the slowness to rush to judgment, and the instinct to nurture people on which so much of childrearing, education, and healing have depended, women are bound to risk overindulging male egos and not standing up for their own rights. How much better it would be if men could muster the subtlety to offer women a love that was protective and caring without being patronizing or disabling. How much better it would be if, as equals, men and women got into a flow of mutual caring and mutual challenging, so that both could be receptive and critical. We are not going to overcome in a generation the patterns developed throughout centuries, nor are we going to outrun our bodies and our hormones. But right now we could speak more frankly to one another, in both admiration and criticism, and we could play together much better.

$\sim$ 8 $\sim$

Men

IF I AM TO LOVE OTHER MEN AS I
love myself, I shall have to show them many of the same things
I want to show women. My analysis of love of the self, both embodied and spiritual, suggested that a tender care is often the
prime desideratum. There is no reason this should not be true
for men's love of one another. Just as one can rightly add that
love of self also has to include discipline and challenge, one can
rightly add that good male friends keep one another on their
toes. But, at the core of the male friendships I most treasure, as
at the core of the love I received from my father and think I experience from Christ, is an acceptance both gentle and unconditional. My father did not push me faster than I wanted to go,
perhaps because he observed that I was already pushing myself.
Christ has been patient in the extreme with my neglect and stu-

pidity, never overbearing. My best friends do tell me the truth. They do speak up when they think I am wrong. But the wider context always makes it clear that whether or not I accept what they have to say, they will continue to love me.

Spurred by the task of writing this book, I have thought about the characterization of men as most crippled by an inability to name their feelings. Women frequently voice this characterization, and now and then so do men. I think men have been making some progress with this problem, no doubt in part due to the sorts of groups I disparaged earlier, but we have many miles to go. One index is the rarity of easy exchanges of personal information and feelings among male acquaintances. If my experience is representative, even men I know quite well speak much more about their work than their hopes and fears, much more about educational theory or theology than about what they long for with their students or what troubles them at prayer.

The healthy male taciturnity that I mentioned previously can explain some of this phenomenon, but by no means the whole. As much as most men, I turn silent when I feel others are trying to hype up my emotions or get me to describe my feelings because it would be interesting. I feel fortunate in having been trained to discern the spirits working in me, and to have received an education that highlighted interiority. I have enjoyed many benefits from having been formed by childhood experiences toward quiet and introspection. So, I judge that if a man who has had much less opportunity to come to know himself and own up to his own feelings finds personal discussion difficult, he deserves a lot of sympathy. Often he gets this sympathy from women, and as long as they do not baby or flatter him, they do him a great service.

Too many of my intimate talks with men have occurred when they had had too much to drink, and yet, even at those times, I have felt that getting their fears out was worth the liabilities. I remember stopping my grammar school shop teacher in his

tracks by asking him whether he thought people were more or
less truthful when drunk. Ten-year-old kids were not supposed
to ask such questions, were not supposed to need to know.

I think one of the things boys most need from men is assurance that the men once found sex troubling, just as the boys
now are experiencing. I think kids have the right to adults' respect—to being told the truth, apologized to when it is appropriate, taken seriously, and even to know that adults need them
and would feel that half of life's light had gone out were the
kids not around.

I have often thought about what I owe my niece, who is now
eleven years old, and recently I have started thinking about
what I owe my nephew, who is charging toward four. When he
first met me, he let me pick him up, because he was used to that
from people my size, but it took several days before he would
turn his head toward me. "You've got my body," he was saying, "but you've got to show you're worthy of my trust." I do
not fear the task of earning his trust, because I believe that all
anyone rightly can ask of us is honesty and love, that these are
what we want to give, more often than not, and that, when we
do give them, things usually turn out well. After being in my
arms in a swimming pool for half an hour or so, my nephew fell
sound asleep. No doubt this was more simple fatigue than any
grand act of trust, but it completed his stealing of my heart.

With nephews and male friends, as with nieces and the wom-
en we love, the trick is having our hearts stolen. Love is a willing despoliation. Ideally, we know what we are letting happen,
but we also feel drawn by a Spirit with purposes beyond our
ken. I know my nephew could turn out to be a bounder, a rot-
ter, all those other things the British public school system has eloquently named. I doubt that he will, but even if he did, his
stealing my heart should only help him. The prejudice in his favor that my love gives him should not mean I would turn my
eyes from evidence of bad character or bad habits. It should not
mean I would in the least countenance his doing drugs or not

working in school. But it should keep any problems such as this, as well as any successes he has, in perspective: framed by the gift of new life he made plain to me, the sacred benefaction he bestowed by letting me into his trust.

Friendship and care between adult men, of course, are more complicated, but many of the verities about trust remain. In listening to friends out of work grope toward acknowledging how demoralized they feel, I have found myself praying to be faithful to their confessions. In reflecting on another vaguely unsatisfying lunch with a bright colleague, I have found myself wondering whether we will ever get beyond scholarly notations and the exchange of new ideas. I have also wondered whether I am not more to blame for our superficiality than he, since I groan at the prospect of taking on another of the sets of burdens that intimate knowledge brings.

Love brings burdens—I have not worked this theme very much. Set me as a seal upon your heart, and I cannot so easily dismiss you when you are inconvenient. The impersonality of busy men, and busy women, may bespeak a sort of honesty: I just cannot make the commitment that seeing you whole might entail. Most people who find themselves in the helping professions can recall many times when they knowingly discouraged intimacy. From time to time I think of overtures to which I deliberately did not respond, feeling guilty that few of them came from attractive people. At some point all of us can plead finitude and fatigue, but we probably reach that point much quicker than Jesus, who has put up with so much importunity and neglect from us.

With the men whom I sense providence has sent me, I try to be attentive and trustworthy. I instinctively cut back on the wisecracking and try to listen more from the center. Men's codes are probably as subtle as women's, because most men have less notion of what they are sending. Indeed, by the rules of our game we are not supposed to be sending polysemously. John Wayne says what he thinks, and neither friend nor foe ever gets it wrong. But many men talk more than they listen, often talk to find out what they think. And many men keep a firm defense against thoughts that would lead them to tender places of conscience, or to the hurts that could make them cry. So we usually do business with a brief locking of eyes, a small softening of voice. For the moment, these convey sympathy, solidarity, willingness to be available should more be needed. Then it is back to the upbeat, positive projection that salesmen and clergy have inflicted on the mass of us. Our business has to be going well, showing a profit, because otherwise we would be wimps. I would like to see more positive projection about the grace we are sure God is always giving, and more honest, humorous discussion of the problems we have to solve. I would like to see macho men decisive and reliable, rather than brutal and inconsistent. Just as real men can learn to eat quiche, although I doubt it can ever become their favorite food, so real men can learn that strength means doing what one promises, what one knows is right, what it takes to love other people with at least faint echoes of the way Christ loves them.

~~ 9 ~~

The Church

MY FINAL FOCUS FOR LOVE OF
neighbor is the Christian community. In developing this focus I
do not mean to imply that we should treat those who are not
Christians with any less care and sympathy. Indeed, one of my
touchstones for a healthy ecclesiology is the extent to which the
Christian community is not dusting its own navel, but is trying
to serve the whole world by means of fuller humanization. By
this touchstone, a depressing fraction of church discussions
seem unhealthy.[9]

For Catholic Christianity, the life of God is far more absorbing
than the bickerings of church members. No doubt few commentators would disagree with this thesis, so baldly put, but in practice the majority ignore it. Moreover, the life of God pulses in

all human beings and a major function of the church, in its sacramental ecclesiology, is to signify how the life of God is going on always and everywhere.

Conservatives are quick to denigrate such a starting point, arguing that it minimizes the importance of the church and takes the heart out of missionary activity. There is some danger of such a minimizing, but the more blatant reality is that divinity itself has set the agenda in these terms. If Christians are less than 25 percent of God's people, the explicitly Christian assembly should not hog the theology of the gathering of God's people. In my opinion, what ecclesiology should most be seeking is demonstrations, both lived and theoretical, of the blessings that Christian faith can bring to any culture's search for fuller humanity. As Lonergan noted, theology mediates between faith and culture. The most important invariant of Christian faith is the saving love of God manifested in Jesus Christ, while the most important invariant of culture is human beings' need for meaning and forgiveness. A theology that makes more of the papacy or sexual morality than of these invariants has its head in the bowl.

The church we must love is both the city raised on a hill, showing all people of good will the graciousness of God, and the motley crew of sinners and roustabouts who make the graciousness of God hard to accredit. Ideally, we Christians would treat other people as our equals, giving and receiving from the stores of wisdom both of us had received. We would not speak of chosenness. Any special status we would claim would be fully earned by our demonstrable wisdom and service. Actually, we continue to be embarrassingly chauvinistic, as just about any document from Rome illustrates. Check the footnotes in the document on the norms concerning artificial insemination and other facets of the new bio-sexual technologies. Can any authority quote only itself and expect the world to find it a humble servant, to believe it cares what others think? Do manly authors eschew self-criticism?

And, of course, this authority only compounds its problems when it forbids dissent on all matters where it has pronounced, fallible as well as infallible. Charles Curran's account of his experiences with Rome merely confirms what has long been obvious.[10] The authorities given to us by God think of us, the church general, as children who should be seen (contributing money), but not heard. Worse, they think of us as little cheerleaders, who should happily shake our pompoms to whatever tunes they currently are piping.

And yet, I think we must reckon with the God-givenness of this authority, as we must reckon with the sinfulness the church has always carried, not least in ourselves. I have most been helped to love the real, gnarled, often ugly church by those who focused on the treasures the Spirit still polishes within it. The more I despise the hurt many church officials produce, and their stupid flouting of their own decrees on religious liberty, the more I am amazed that the stream of saintly wisdom, the beauty of Mozart Masses, the reality of self-sacrificing ministry, continue to flow. Bathing in that stream, I am able to forget for a while the detritus thrown up by Christian sinfulness and abuse of authority. God is greater than we who compose the church. The branches have significance only in the measure they serve the vine. Many people who think they are leaving the church never leave the vine. All people who continue to love what the church sometimes has been, and always keeps flickering, can take as their birthright from God the right to speak their minds and vote with their feet.

Despite its many unattractive features, the church continues to mediate God's grace. One of my colleagues in Tulsa is a Jewish teacher of creative writing. She has gotten immersed in the movement for nuclear disarmament, and the community she has sought out makes Catholic priests and sisters her main friends. Another colleague is a cradle Catholic, highly sophisticated and critical, yet always going back to what he learned at the Catholic Worker or from the leaders of the Neo-Thomist revival. Any people seriously interested in spirituality soon look into the world religions, and usually they have a period of fascination with Catholic mysticism. Any people interested in liberating the poor soon run into Latin American liberation theology.

One can argue that the papal dress and pageantry are anachronistic, but one cannot gainsay the fascination they still exert.

What both amuses and pains me in the recent strategies of church authorities is their shocking amnesia. Obviously, the most beloved Christian leader in recent memory was Pope John XXIII, but few church leaders seem to have grasped the reason why John was so loved. So, altogether too much like our recent U.S. presidents, they present the persona of the tough guy. I think John XXIII was the real man, so let me conclude by reflecting briefly on his love for the church.

It was a love full of warmth. It was a love wanting to promote freedom. John's first instinct was not fear, as the first instinct of Paul VI seemed to be. It was not to impose authority, as the first instinct of John Paul II seems to be. It was to convey solidarity, common humanity, the sense that all human beings are in it together. The "it" was God's romance with the world, as John's Christian faith led him to interpret history. The first word from God was yes, and the first word from John was yes.

I realize that John was quite traditional in his piety and that he made no radical break with the traditional papal symbolisms. Far more importantly, however, he broke with the almost hundred year old assumption that all wisdom resides in Rome, and so he opened the church's windows to the rest of the world. Today, one has to sympathize with the burden that he has placed on his successors. He was a very hard act to follow. If we commoners in the church were to take him as seriously as Paul VI and John Paul II have, no doubt he would seem more threatening to us, too. Yet I hope we would still find his first word to be yes, his first instinct to be trust, and the import of these first things the lesson we should place first. Our faith is that God loves us, that God cares for us, that God numbers each hair of any of our heads. Whatever our nationality, race, sex, faith, virtue, wealth, intelligence, God cares more for the divine child he sees within us. Mothering this child, God remains the crux of any viable spirituality, past or present, female or male. Long live God.

Part Four

Making Connections:
Recent Trends
in Spiritualities for Men

≈ 10 ≈

Moving Into Mystery

ONE SELDOM TAKES A PATH ALONE.
This is as true in the area of male spirituality as it is in any other
field. Other men and women approach the topic from different
angles and it seems advisable to engage them in dialogue so that
the emerging trends and important developments can be re-
vealed. Thus, in this final section, I intend to draw on the insights of Martin Pable's *A Man and His God*, James Nelson's *The
Intimate Connection*, and John Sanford and George Lough's *What
Men Are Like*.[11] By exploring what they have said, I hope to
delve more deeply into the central core of a contemporary male
spirituality.

These authors come from a Catholic, a Protestant, and a Jungian psychological approach respectively. All have interesting,
stimulating things to say about men's spiritual needs, and all ev-

idence both considerable experience in dealing with men's groups and considerable sympathy for the problems men face in contemporary Western society.

Before dealing with each of these texts in some detail, let me first reflect on the discipline of pastoral theology, into which they roughly fall. In recent years, pastoral theology has become much influenced by psychology. Generally, this influence has been for the good. Regularly pastoral theology deals with problems of maturation, addiction, self-image, feelings, and blocks. All such problems require a theory of the normal, healthy personality, and a good handle on how mind and heart, will and emotion, ought to conspire. From humanistic psychology has come considerable insights into people's struggles for maturity, as well as considerable warmth in dealing with people's failures.

The major warning that most theologians issue concerning the influence of psychology in pastoral theology is that it not substitute for faith. On its own, psychology usually brackets the question of the existence and influence of God. Neither the operations of the Holy Spirit nor the history of Christian spirituality rightfully appears on the psychologist's agenda. This is not to say that psychologists have not dealt with the existence and influence of God, the operations of the Holy Spirit, and the history of Christian spirituality, sometimes to illumine them considerably. It is to say that if pushed to explain its ultimate criterion for health and sickness, psychology has to bring forward the humanistic judgments that its own experience, reflection, and theorizing have produced. It cannot invoke texts of Scripture, documents of the church, or opinions of leading saints. All such religious authorities begin with a commitment of faith (in Jesus and God's revelation through him) that falls outside the psychologist's pale.

Pastoral theologians who employ psychological insights need not denature either faith or psychology. Ideally, they have found tools for explaining how faith, hope, and love tend to operate, why encouragement seems to produce more virtue than punishment does, how people can share their feelings and so liberate their religious imaginations and hopes, and so forth. On the other hand, if the books that I have surveyed for this dialogue are representative, theological depth is not the strong point of current pastoral theology, at least when it grapples with the question of a spirituality for men. Nelson's book, which reflects his own standing as a solid theologian, does better than the other two, but even it is more interested in the affective side of such topics as mortality and sexuality than in their theological significance.

Probably the best lesson for a theologian to draw from this state of affairs is one that nurtures humility. If obviously well-intentioned pastoral theologians have not found the work of doctrinal or speculative theologians directly relevant to their counseling, preaching, giving of retreats, and the like, maybe something is wrong with much doctrinal and speculative theology. (Biblical theology seems to fare better, perhaps because so often it is merely illumining a relatively concrete and affective scriptural text. Moral theology stands on the side of doctrinal and speculative theology, apparently too specialized or abstract an affair to convert very directly into pastoral usage.) Alternatively, the doctrinal or speculative theologian might wonder whether in moving toward spirituality he or she should not place more emphasis on the mysteriousness of the divine realities being discussed and less emphasis on the categories in which either Christian tradition or recent speculation has sought to bring those realities within human purview. Such a shift of emphasis need not imply that, for its own specialized tasks and services, either doctrinal or speculative theology is inadequate or malformed. Both, as presently practiced, might be judged to do a fine job at the specialized tasks of presenting what Christian understanding of given doctrines has been and how such doctrines may best be thought to cohere today. The point rather would be what shifts of emphasis seem necessary if one is to make doctrine and speculation illumine people's holistic, spiritual lives.

My opinion, as implied, is that doctrine becomes most helpful for spiritual nourishment when it becomes "mystagogic." This

word, which has a venerable traditional usage among the
church fathers, implies that one is evoking, summoning, point-
ing to the divine mystery of God. It takes seriously the many
dicta of faith to the effect that God never comes under our control, loving the distinction that Aquinas, for instance, makes between knowing that God exists and knowing what God is. We
can know that God exists, because of the testimony of Scripture
and tradition, as well as the congruence of God's existence with
the data of human experience. Inasmuch as such data cry out for
a source of being and order transcendent to their own finitude,
mortality, lack of self-sufficiency, and lack of intelligibility, they
make the testimony of faith reasonable. So, to hold that God exists can be defended as sane, pious, and altogether a healthy
way of handling the deepest questions about the world's foundations.

On the other hand, as soon as we try to say what God is, we
run into great problems. Any such effort uses images, words,
concepts, and judgments that are limited by their origins in finite minds, experiences, and group sharings. All of the tools one
can employ in dealing with predication about God fail to measure up to the limitless character of what they set to work upon.
Even the negative tools that come into play, like the word "limitless" that I used in the prior sentence, cannot claim to capture
the divine or render it flawlessly. Such a tool depends at least
tacitly on a human experience and understanding of a limit, a
boundary, something that sets a term and so defines a reality.
What it means to exist without boundaries, as a positive mode
of being, is very unclear. Even to speak of a "mode" of being,
when one is dealing with God, introduces distortions, because
God is a simple fullness of existence, rather than existence chan-
neled into a particular conduit.

Scripture, revelation, the Incarnation of the Logos, and the
other mainstays of the Christian construction of a sense of God
and ultimate reality do not remove this problem. They provide
believers with privileged symbols, ciphers of the divine that are
thought to work better than alternatives from outside the Christian band of experience, but they never remove the mysterious-

ness of the divine being. Nothing human can. For human beings, God is intrinsically mysterious. To be God and to be unin-
telligible go hand in hand.

Such unintelligibility, to be sure, is a matter of fullness rather
than of deficiency. One could say that primal matter is unintelli-
gible, but only because there is nothing in it for the mind to fathom. The problem with God is just the reverse. There is too much
light, too much intelligibility for the mind to fathom. Thus even
the person of Christ, or the words of Scripture, or the utterances
of infallible papal declarations, do not remove the mysteriousness of God. The beatific vision of God itself does not remove
the divine mystery (which is why the objection that heaven
would be boring is fatuous). Always God is greater. Always
there is more to know, love, and worship.

I believe that spirituality is most nourishing when it finds
ways to bring the mystery, and so the living presence of God, to
bear on people's consciousness, their awareness. God is always
present to people's being and hearts, because without God's
presence nothing would exist or be holy. Yet most of the time
we are not aware of the divine presence. It impresses itself
upon us obliquely, implicitly, in darkness. A great deal of the
better literature dealing with Christian prayer boils down to
helpful instruction in how to deal with a God we cannot understand. Such instruction amounts to arguing, demonstrating, that
we can love beyond what we know. Because God has taken the
initiative, we can abide in dark nights and clouds of unknowing,
letting our hearts respond to what our minds cannot conceive.

This conviction, that we can love beyond what we know, will
do much to shape my response to the three books that will be
used to stimulate discussion in the following chapters. Regularly, I shall be using the mystagogic core of traditional doctrinal
and speculative theology to counter what I consider a religious
superficiality in these books. I might add that I consider them
representative of mainstream pastoral theology and so am interested in them as much for their typical characteristics as for their
particular insights and oversights.

❧ 11 ❧

Spirituality and Holism

IN THE STRUGGLE TO DEVELOP A
male spirituality for today, two of the emerging trends are to
see, more and more clearly, that men do have an innate hunger
for God, not just for a sense of well-being, and that spirituality
needs to be broken out of isolation and connected to every important aspect of a man's life. These trends are important steps
forward. They deserve our careful consideration and further development, and the best way to begin, I think, is by turning to
one of their clearest expositions—Martin Pable's *A Man and His
God.*

A Man and His God has the great virtue of stemming from
Pable's considerable experience as a counselor and retreat master. It begins by making the case that many men feel neglected

by their churches, inasmuch as such churches seem to consider "spirituality" something for women. Pable stresses the need that all people have for a religious or spiritual vision, and he makes a good case that many of men's frustrations stem from their lacking such a vision. When their work or family life seems to have run dry, the most likely reason is that they have little purchase on their feelings, little attunement to the movements of the Spirit in their depths. This in turn implies a criticism of the religious fare they have either been given or been able to receive. To remedy this situation, Pable has written a simple book detailing the insights to which his pastoral experience of men's spiritual problems has led him.

First, he has found it useful to deal with the question of self-identity. If men will ask themselves who they in fact are (or if they will raise to reflective awareness the modes this question already is taking in their lives), they usually will find that they are dissatisfied with the answers that society at large has been providing them. Society at large tends to define a man in terms of his job. Anyone doubting this has only to measure the loss of identity and self-esteem that unemployment regularly brings to men in the United States. Without a job telling them who they are and how they fit into their society, most men are quite lost. Other parts of the typical male's self-identity come from the advertising media, which project ideals of athleticism, good looks, chic clothing, ease with women, competitiveness, and so on. Little in the public image of U.S. men provides for interiority, tenderness, not caring about sports, and identifying with the poor or society's "losers. " In other words, there is little provision for traits one might find in the evangelical Christ. At the least, then, asking about his identity can lead a man to question the superficiality of most of the images he has imbibed. As well, it can suggest the possibility of a better set of images and criteria, one both easier to achieve and more responsive to deeper parts of his male selfhood.

Pable next deals with such key concerns of anyone's life as balancing work and leisure, finding love, assuming adult responsibilities, and fashioning a program for ongoing spiritual growth. His own summary of his findings stresses the need he has observed in men for interiority, holism, and regular recourse to prayer and the sacraments. I shall have something to say about each of these headings, so let me conclude this sketch by noting the perhaps novel plea that Pable makes for the typical male Catholic's engagement in evangelization. Referring to Pope Paul VI's encyclical on evangelization, Pable makes the case that a faith fully alive naturally wants to share the good news in which it delights. Precisely how the average layman should work at evangelization will vary from situation to situation, but in arguing that spreading the faith is an important ingredient of any adequate male spirituality, Pable has done his readers the favor of concretizing the challenges that spirituality ought to be setting them.

Pable's style is easygoing and anecdotal. He intersperses sizeable quotations from Scripture and makes passing reference both to books suitable for further reading and to items of popular culture. This style has set me an interesting problem: if this style is suitable for most men, my own concerns (or at least the way I tend to express them) might be too difficult to grasp, and many men would miss them. The problem, then, is the same that faces the undergraduate college teacher: how much to accommodate and how much to try to draw one's hearers beyond where they begin? What I am going to call Pable's relatively low quotient of theological or spiritual insight therefore may be an act of wisdom or prudence. Perhaps he has deliberately decided that the mystery of God or the blazing character of the iconic Christ will not fly, cannot be communicated to most male readers. Or, perhaps he has employed the Pauline insight into the variety of gifts that writers possess and decided that his gifts lie in simplicity, staying within the boundaries of common sense, and using the terms supplied most men by popular U.S. culture. That hypothesis pleases me, if only because it suggests that I can try to proffer other literary gifts, under the hope that they may serve other parts of the male audience.

To illustrate Pable's style and main theses, let me quote from the beginning of his concluding chapter:

Throughout this book I have been making two basic assumptions. One is that..."real men do have a spirituality." That is, there are a lot of males in our society who are not satisfied with pursuing The Great American Dream: wealth, status, success, power, or whatever. They either know intuitively or have learned by experience that the dream is more illusion than reality, at least in its capacity to provide genuine happiness and fulfillment. So these men are looking for something deeper, something they may not always name. But they know it has more to do with inner reality than with outward appearance, something more spiritual than material. We have named it "spirituality," and we defined it as "the ongoing endeavor to grow in our relationship with God." We saw that "spiritual growth" means forming a view of reality based on God's word in scripture and developing a lifestyle, making decisions, in light of that vision.

The second assumption is that spirituality is not just a head trip or a cozy feeling of being on good terms with God. It has to connect with and influence all the important aspects of a man's life. That's why we devoted whole chapters to the areas of work and leisure, friendship and marriage, and the exercise of responsibility. We tried to catch something of God's vision for these human realities and what kind of responses we may be called to make.

In this final chapter I will be making a third assumption: namely, that spirituality is never a once-and-for-all achievement. Rather, it is a process of ongoing growth change and response to new challenges. [12]

In response to Pable's good summary of his views, I am moved first to add that men (and women: little in that summary is specific to men) hunger for an interior life, a closer relation with God, because God is always luring them toward this. The drive of human consciousness is toward increased understanding and love. The only adequate term of this drive is divinity itself: unlimited being and goodness. In addition, the actions of God attributed by Scripture and tradition to the Holy Spirit suggest that this natural drive of human consciousness has been personalized by God's personal overtures. The God who has not called us servants but friends deals with us in the coin of friendship: mutual concern, warmth, interest. The Spirit whom Paul has making our deepest prayer, with sighs too deep for words, has so identified with our needs and cause that we can say, quite strictly, that in our deepest prayer God is praying to God. And this is but a form, an expression, of the New Testament's view that the Spirit is working our divinization. We are becoming sharers of the divine nature, through the movements of Christ's Spirit in our hearts.

What Jesus was for his disciples—their advocate or defender—the Spirit has been since the time of Jesus' ascent to the Father. The deepest levels of the Christian doctrine of grace therefore are trinitarian. When human beings know and love to any significant degree, they are serving as carriers, conduits, of the Son and Spirit who express the infinite knowing and love of the Godhead. I find none of this language in Pable, or the other two authors we shall treat. As I mentioned earlier, that may be an act of wisdom on their part, if in fact this language means nothing to the average American male. But some negotiation would seem to be in order, lest that average male be condemned to do without the innermost imagery of the Christian spiritual life. Let me therefore try to exemplify what the doctrine of grace may mean in experiential terms, hoping that my examples will give specificity as well as depth to the thesis that many men are longing for greater meaning in their lives.

Men who reach middle age inevitably think about aging and death. The statistics about heart disease and cancer are one prod to such thought, especially when those statistics come home to roost among one's family and friends. Another prod is the obsession of our culture with youth, particularly as this finds expression in curiosity about sexual performance. Men who hear that males reach their sexual peak at age nineteen and thereafter decline may smile and make jokes, but few over forty will escape twitches of anxiety. The further message that women tend to reach their sexual peak about age thirty, when combined with the tendency of men to marry women several years younger than themselves, only compounds such anxiety.

Third, there are the signs, the reasons to reflect, that come not from the outside media but from one's own body. The seven minute mile gets harder and harder. After a hard week's work the prospect of a weekend of hard partying can be frightening. So slowly, nearly inevitably, men tend to slow down, mellow, and become more reflective. Gradually they begin to catch up with women, who typically have been more reflective all along. The religious question is how to capitalize on these dynamics, and most pastoral theologians seem to answer it by suggesting that the time may be ripe for a retreat, or joining a men's group, or setting aside more time for prayer. Such a suggestion is fine in itself, but it can pass over the opportunity to discuss the typical patterns of spiritual development.

From many traditions, East and West, we know that middle age regularly serves as a time for appropriating one's tradition. Ideally one would have received an intense religious formation as a youth. But such a formation perforce could only be rather intellectual, because one did not have sufficient experience to understand what the great truths of one's tradition meant for daily living. Having a family, working for a living, seeing at first hand the corruption of the institutions society everywhere establishes, and realizing one's own share in such corruption all tend to sober the enthusiasm and assurance one developed as a youth. In the Christian case, old teachings about sin and grace may now burst into relevance. Now the sin of the world ("original sin") may seem one of the most profound analyzes of human disorder ever to have arisen.

If so, the relevance of Christ should be equally plain. The Kingdom of God that Jesus preached may now appear to be nothing less than the overthrow of the reign of sin dominant since the rise of human consciousness (the "Fall" of Adam and

Eve). The vice that goes on at one's place of work, the graft and adultery, can come into clearer focus, seeming both less surprising and more deforming. On the other hand, the virtue that one finds among colleagues who are honest and do their work with no fanfare can gain a third dimension, now coming to seem marvelous, a sign of God's grace.

One can imagine a similar analysis of what men experience at home. Especially relevant would be the increased appreciation of the sweetness of one's children, the fidelity of one's wife, the fact that food and shelter are not items of worry. Less and less do maturing men take for granted such simple things as a good family life, good health, decent colleagues at work. More and more they sense the frailty of all human accomplishments, if only because more and more they sense the frailty of their own bodies. They are ripe for explanations of this experience, and the best such explanations, I believe, treat it as a mercy of the Holy Spirit. What maturation ought to be working is a detachment that the Spirit can use to expand one's horizons, to increase one's appreciation of the precisely religious insight that God, on whom the entire order of creation hinges, is a being of a completely different order. God is not a thing. Though all flesh is but grass, though the grass withers and the flowers fade, the Word of God endures forever.

For Christians, Jesus is this Word of God incarnate. He gives a human face, a human touch, to the imperishable expression of God that can save us from the nothingness built into our mortality, from the twistedness couched in our sin. The personal relationship that Pable winningly wants to foster with God ought to take a man's perceptions of frailty and strength alike and make them the focus of a twofold exchange. With words, petitions, clear images, traditional prayers, a man may send toward Christ, the human face of God, all his worries and all his thanksgiving. He ought also to be told, however, that his sighs too deep for words have always ascended to the Father, because of the movement of the Spirit in his depths. He need not attend to the Spirit clearly. It is enough that he has tried to love the life given to him, accepting its hardships and feeling grateful for its beauty. The more he can settle into such a holistic prayer, seconding the simple movement of the Spirit that gathers up the whole of his life and takes it toward the Father, the less artificial prayer will seem. Just as a mature man knows that the best times with his wife and children surpass anything he can put into words, so a man whose prayer is maturing knows that the main business of prayer is sharing with God, being to being, from the center of himself toward the round fullness of the divine mystery.

Pable's second assumption, that spirituality ought to deal with and affect all the significant dimensions of a man's life, is right on the mark. In another work I have spoken of the "holistic" spirituality such an assumption sponsors.[13] There my argument was that love is the core energy of the spiritual life, and that love has a tendency, one might even say a desire, to warm and deepen our work as well as our prayer, our relations with nature and our bodies as well as our relations with our friends and lovers. Any division of our lives into work and prayer, family life and life outside the home, physical pursuits and mental pursuits, finally breaks down and is shown to be artificial. We are wholes, even as we feel the impress of nature, society, the divine mystery, our bodies, the revelations and the needs of other people. Consequently, we need a spirituality that honors and advances our wholeness.

The Catholic Christian view of creation and grace offers the foundations for just such a spirituality. Creation ought to remind us of God's largess in sharing being outside of the divine nature. Indeed, we ought mainly to think in terms of the refrain of Genesis: God saw that it was very good. Grace deepens this positive outlook, reminding us that God has wanted to share divinity itself with us, and that this divine desire was willing to mount the cross. If God so loved us and our world that God gave the only begotten Son for our salvation, how can God fail to give us all the lesser gifts in the divine treasury?

I find this lyrical faith more powerful than the chants of humanistic psychology about self-affirmation, because it comes with biblical warrant and seems objective. No doubt, one can make a good case for self-affirmation, if only by glossing the biblical command to love others as we love ourselves. It is also true that Scripture is not so objective as past generations, or fundamentalists of the present generation, tend to depict it. Everything written for our instruction passed through the psyche of a human collaborator and reflected that person's need for holism and integration. Still, the Christian tradition has always accorded Scripture a certain independence of human craft and need.

The proof of this independence is that startling ability of Scripture to draw us up short and remind us of perspectives that worldlings seldom see. The most profound of these is the fate of Jesus. What happened when God's love took flesh ought to sober all readers. Paul called Christ on the cross the power and wisdom of God because he saw that God's love could only triumph paradoxically. If it were to respect human freedom, it had to endure rejection, even blasphemy. By embracing such sin, and showing itself stronger by resurrecting the Christ, God's love put a new thing into the world. Henceforth it would be dramatically obvious that the greatest force in the universe is the love that can create something from the cold nothingness of hatred. If we conjecture that God's love is the ultimate explanation for the Big Bang and the existence of the physical universe, we can trump that conjecture by concluding that Christ on the cross represents explosive creativity in the moral order. At least once, God showed that rejection cannot be the final word. Whatever those who crucified Jesus intended, in fact they occasioned a demonstration of the divine insistence that the darkness would never comprehend the light of God's desire to take human beings to the divine bosom.

How does this relate to holism? Quite directly. If Jesus crucified and resurrected represents the center of the Christian's moral universe, then nothing to which human beings put their hand cannot become sacramental. By securing the Incarnation and showing that Christ was the victor over the forces that willed his destruction, God has given us warrant for considering every person and thing we meet a potential friend. The disorder that petrifies the world ignorant of the resurrection has been torn up by its roots. However long and difficult the spread of the implications of Christ's resurrection, believers can rejoice and feel that nothing can separate them from the love of God. I would specify this "nothing" as meaning "nothing at work, " "nothing read in the newspapers," "nothing experienced with one's children," "nothing experienced from one's enemies," and much more. Nothing really ought to mean *nothing*: a complete devastation of the power of evil to threaten our foundations. If God is for us as the resurrection proclaims, who of significance can be against us? Holistic spirituality is the edifice we build when we understand the radical reaches of the divine will to secure love "for us men and our salvation."

I wish the typical discussion of prayer and the sacraments would use more of such Pauline and creedal language. When we urge men to pray regularly, we ought to assure them that the heart of the matter is simply showing up, making the effort to commune with God in confidence that God has loved us unconditionally, and wanting to open our hearts to the challenges and consolations of the divine mystery. Certainly it is useful to speak about using vocal prayers like mantras, to fix the upper levels of one's attention and free the depths of one's spirit for romance with God. Certainly discussing meditation and contemplation can bear great fruit. But these remain in the order of means or technique. The order of ends and substance focuses on God's being more intimate to us than we are to ourselves, on God's being greater than our hearts, even when they condemn us, on God's being, like the father of the prodigal son, better than we could ever appreciate.

Prayer is the celebration of such central articles of our faith and the lamentation of the fear, thickness, and sin that keep us from exulting in them every day. Were we formed by such a faith, our work and human relations would take wing. We would feel warmed to our marrow, and from this warmth could only come a new creativity that drew from the freshness of creation the divine love-life itself. Everyone knows that when we are in love the world seems beautiful, we can put up with fools, and our enemies seem more to be pitied and helped than feared.

Everyone knows that peak experiences traffic in such deep and subtle passages that one's sense of well-being itself becomes a psalm of praise. Let men catch some of the fire of Christ's own love, some of the ardor of the risen Christ flashing from the pages of Revelation, and they will understand, at least for the nonce, why all the saints were passionate prayers. The saints could not get enough of God, because God was so beautiful, so profound, so real, so complete an antidote for the artificial, depressing aspects of human experience.

Take the man on the verge of burnout, worn thin by the demands of a job he has outgrown or a homelife that has honed in on material possessions or a circle of friends who offer few challenges. If some good pastor could show him the bracing powers of simple prayer, he might come to cherish quiet stretches in a darkened church, on his knees before a flickering vigil light, as the restoration of his lost spirit. The quiet could compensate for all the babble that has been grinding him down. The depths of the darkness could compensate for the superficiality of much of the work he must do, the entertainment to which he is exposed, the goals he is offered. True, when he left the church he might have to compromise, for the sake of meeting longstanding obligations. Nonetheless, for a while he probably could take such compromise with a touch of grace and humor: how silly we human beings usually are, how fixated on things of no account.

Frequenting the sacraments might bring this same liberating experience. The bread of life, so simple yet limitless in its symbolism of God's nurture of us, puts all discussion of food and money in proper perspective. The sacrament of penance makes human conflict penultimate, relieving the depression that marital strife or the strife of the nations tends to create. Final anointing seals the whole notion of our passage through time, telling the middle-aged man, increasingly conscious of his mortality, that what afflicts the body is secondary, what anneals and strengthens the spirit is primary. And so with the other sacraments.

The point is that both prayer and reception of the sacraments concretize God's coming to us incarnationally. When the Spirit gives us the grace to see and feel their significance, they seem both utterly natural and utterly extraordinary. Gradually, we sense what the saints meant when they said that everything is grace. We could not have been, yet here we are, enduring to an increasingly ripe age. We could have gone so far astray that we never found our way back, and yet even when we were sinners God loved us. We could have burned out, trusting our own resources and refusing to open ourselves to the divine darkness, and yet here we remain, hunched over our pew, or taking our walk by the sea, again experiencing the lift of the Spirit that throws depression and fatigue behind, that engages us with the ever ancient, ever new mystery of why there is something rather than nothing, why God has given us Christ as an unfailing source of hope.

∾ 12 ∾

Sexuality, Friendship, and a New Sexuality

As I HAVE USED MARTIN PABLE'S book to stimulate further thoughts about emerging trends in a contemporary spirituality for men, so shall I use James Nelson's work, *The Intimate Connection*. Nelson delves into the connection between male sexuality and male spirituality. His analyses reflect not only his standing as a trained professor of theology, but also his involvement with men's groups. Psychology plays a strong role in his diagnoses of men's needs and problems—in many ways a stronger role than theology. Yet his book is informed throughout by his strong faith. It is one of the better pastoral approaches to men's spirituality that I have seen, and if forced to rank the three books I am considering here I would place Nelson's first. Let me indicate the convictions with which

Nelson begins his study, and his style, before suggesting where
I find the book wanting.

Nelson begins by sketching a picture of U.S. males' mental
and physical health that is not encouraging: men die earlier than
women, have higher rates of suicide, show more chemical de-
pendency, more often go to prison, and more often suffer vio-
lent deaths. Beyond these statistics Nelson finds widespread
hurting:

> It is found in our yearning for emotional intimacy with
> other males—sons, fathers, and friends—yet finding our-
> selves unprepared, unequipped, and fearful of that inti-
> macy. The hurt is in our wanting relationships of genu-
> ine equality and mutuality with women, yet finding
> ourselves crippled by centuries of male sexism and by
> our emotional dependencies on the opposite sex. The
> hurt is in our discovery that we have bought heavily into
> the message that our self-worth is directly dependent
> upon our occupational success, and yet the idol of work
> somehow does not deliver its promised salvation.
>
> ... I suspect that men who read books such as this are, as
> I am, not only hurting but deeply yearning. We are
> yearning for closer, more fulfilling, more life-giving con-
> nectedness with others, with our world, and with our-
> selves. This means we are yearning for closer connected-
> ness with God, the heart of the universe itself. When we
> yearn for life-giving relationships with any person or
> part of creation, we are at the very same time reaching
> for God. For, according to an incarnational faith, God is
> the spiritual presence who becomes incarnate in and
> through creaturely flesh. Another way of saying this is
> that we are simply longing for more life-giving connect-
> edness between our sexuality and our spirituality.[14]

Nelson proposes to explore men's hurting, and possible healing, under five headings: sexual mystery, friendship, mortality,

masculinity, and new paths for a sexual spirituality. His message under the first four headings is that men mainly need to embrace these aspects of their human condition, treating them positively as sources of fulfillment. In his final chapter, Nelson suggests various new and positive emphases on sexuality that have been bringing it out of the shadows and making it more central to the life of the Christian community than previously it had been. I find his closing analysis very hopeful, and I agree that viewing sexuality positively, seeing it as more relational and rooted in the core of a person's self, moving away from a concentration on individual sexual acts, and the like, should all create a healthier Christian community.

My main worry is that Nelson has misplaced his hopes. Relatively little in his book deals with the Christ who is the power and wisdom of God, or the Holy Spirit who makes Christians' prayer. Little, in fact, is said about prayer, the imitation of Christ, the function of grace to heal wounded personalities, or the divine life into which God would take our fearful mortality. It is instructive that Nelson's use of "incarnational" in the section we quoted makes no mention of Christ. I do not think he would deny the significance of Christ in the Christian understanding of the enfleshment of grace, yet his instinctive option for a unitarian or psychological sense of incarnation shortchanges Christian tradition. Neither the Scriptures nor the sacraments speak such a diminished language. For both, grace is a function of Jesus the Christ, the one to whom Eastern Orthodoxy loves to pray as "Christ our God."

Once again the question arises: is this choice of non-theological language deliberate, made in virtue of considerable experience that such language means little to the majority of men nowadays? Or does it represent an inadvertent deflection from a tradition, especially a sacramental and mystical tradition, that the author has too little plumbed? Nelson would have to answer these questions for himself, but my suspicion is that he has given traditional Christian theology and spirituality too cursory a hearing.

Predictably enough, my own view is that the transformation

spoken of in such traditional theology and spirituality is far more profound than the transformations one can deal with psychologically. To be sure, religious transformation has an important psychological component, and traditional theology often was both poorer and more impotent than it need have been because it did not appreciate how the human psyche is best nourished. It also seems true to say that many of the masters of Christian spirituality instinctively appreciated the need to heal sexuality by positive assurances and get people beyond guilt and self-concern.

My point is not to disparage psychology, least of all when it shows how the mercy, the kindness, the healing touch of God is best mediated. My point rather is to suggest that the claims of Christian tradition break out of the horizon most psychology assumes. The alienation that grace would overcome is far more profound than that between the sexes, or between the individual's reason and affection. The sinful alienation that grace would overcome certainly manifests itself in problems between the sexes or discomforts in the individual, but its more profound thrust is toward the destruction of meaning and joy themselves. By narrowing human beings' attention to themselves and their tiny span of history, sins of pride, self-concern, or narcissism block out the great realities of the gratuity of creation, the unthinkably good news of salvation, the defeat of all human despair in Christ's resurrection, the fulfillment of the best human intuitions about community in the Trinity, and much more.

Are these perspectives of faith merely notional entities, possessing no experiential foundation? Karl Rahner certainly did not think so. He argued eloquently that grace changes a person's horizon, a person's sense of reality, even when that person has little ability to articulate how. For example, many people of faith experience that the nothingness into which all considerations of ultimacy, or all pursuits of the foundations of consciousness, run, is a too-fullness. They find it relatively easy to accept the fact that they will never understand God, because of God's infinite intelligibility, and it is not hard for them to correlate this infinity with contemplative experiences at prayer. The opaqueness that attends any direct address of God precisely as God somehow seems entirely appropriate. Equally appropriate seem the theses that love can go where insight cannot, and that the Holy Spirit is responsible for making the opaqueness or darkness of contemplative prayer congenial.

Now, it is entirely true that one cannot prove these interpretations of fairly common religious experiences. They depend on faith, meaning by that a trust in the God spoken of by Scripture and tradition. It is also true that many psychological interpretations of inner experiences depend on faith in the particular psychological system (for example, the Jungian) being used. The difference in the commitments remains significant, however, because religious faith by definition focuses on a God bound to defeat human understanding. Thus such faith implies the human being's need, finally, to say yes or no to a life never fully understood, a self never fully chosen. Faith in a particular theory, psychological or other, does not entail such ultimacy. That is why I find truly religious faith more important than views about the psyche or psychosexual development.

A last word about specifically Christian faith, before we take up the particular topics Nelson treats as the crucial aspects of male existence (the existential features with which men have to come to grips, if they are to gain wholeness and happiness). Specifically, Christian faith trusts that Jesus' embodiment of divine love is the best guide to a successful life. It finds in the words, deeds, and attitudes of Jesus its model for grappling with both sorrow and joy, both pain and exaltation. Nothing is preferable to the example of Jesus—as living experience of Jesus as a risen Lord, through private prayer and communal worship, brings that example alive. Psychological insights may be very precious, but no Christian spirituality of my liking is ever going to substitute them for the image and impact of Jesus himself. Indeed, it might seem ludicrous to suggest such a substitution, were there not so many books on the market that either directly or indirectly propose it. The few directly proposing it argue that psychological categories best translate the intentions of traditional biblical and theological language. The many indirectly proposing it argue by inadvertence: Jungian or other categories get the lion's share of attention, while Jesus is treated as a tag-a-long. That seems to me precisely an inversion of the order that ought to prevail.

Granted the theological limits of his ambitions, Nelson does a good job of exposing the positive allure of sexuality, the problems of male friendship, and the significance of accepting one's mortality. Concerning sexuality, he reminds us that we never can fathom what our sexuality means, because it is an inseparable part of our whole being or selfhood. I would say that whatever pastoral theology can do to increase our appreciation of the fusion of sexuality and selfhood is almost certain to pay rich dividends. Not only will it help us cast off the negative views of sexuality too often purveyed by religion, it also will help us advance a Christian eros.

Eros is the love of beauty, the response to the splendor of other people, God's world, and divinity itself. I have spoken of eros at some length in the first part of this book. Here I would only repeat that until we have fallen in love with God, and at least a few other human beings, we won't comprehend the energy and joy of the saints, nor their possible analogues for the rest of us. The play and pleasure of mature sexuality is something so good in its fruits that it must have a primal form of being in God.

Christian imagery for the Godhead has yet to take full account of what eros might mean for the eternal processions of Son and Spirit, yet the clues one can find in the theologies of other religions (for example, Judaism, Hinduism, Buddhism, and Chinese religion) suggest that the God who playfully ordered the universe is full of an intimate love of beauty, a selfless desire for union, a fertile warmth that makes whatever it touches come into being, increase, and prosper. I think that encouraging erotic love in men therefore means encouraging something central to their imaging of God. Inasmuch as men regularly focus their eros on women, it means encouraging men to consider women partners to a relationship that evokes the blessed life of the divine persons themselves. Inasmuch as men regularly focus their eros on their work, it means encouraging men to think of their work as an imitation, or continuance, of the processes through which God initially brought the universe into being and continues to conserve it.

Masculine friendship comes up for discussion in most books about men, often in the form of a dirge about the rarity with which men share their feelings and show one another their most debilitating fears or most tender hopes. The camaraderie that men can develop sometimes gets good marks, but a model of women's easy sharing of feelings tends to relegate such camaraderie to second class status. Most commentators also note the fear among heterosexual men that close friendships will be considered homosexual. All in all, then, men are judged to have a hard time achieving satisfactory, profound friendships with other men. I myself concurred in this judgment, though now the considerable literature from ancient Greece and other cultures in praise of male friendship gives me pause.

More importantly, however, my sense is that friendship of the sort most helpful to Christian spirituality only emerges when the friends share their faith. Here my assumption is that faith, or at least grappling with questions of sin and grace, as these concretely present themselves in experience, is at the heart of Christians' efforts to make their way through time. I don't mean "faith" to connote anything pious or artificial. I simply mean that Christian existence entails living at a deeper level than what one's salary, hobbies, and the yield from last night's television create. Unless one somehow delves into such questions as how to gain lasting peace of soul, how to recall the moments of joy that gave spark to one's spiritual hopes, and how to deepen one's sense of gratitude for forgiveness, one's friendship is bound to be superficial.

I think the precisely religious problem in the typical U.S. man's friendships is our awkwardness in speaking about our experiences of God. Secular commentators might argue that this is merely a subspecies of our general reluctance to deal with our emotions, but I think something more is at work. By opening the issue of God we have to admit that we are interested in or troubled by "big questions," and that we may be quite amateur at something one could consider the main expertise marking a mature personality. Certainly in most traditional cultures the mark of the elder and sage was knowledge of the sacred mysteries by which the tribe oriented itself. The secularism of modern culture, combined with the unattractive features of fundamentalist religious know-it-alls, has discouraged most men from considering religious wisdom a manly pursuit. Yet serious Christians have to admit, in their heart of hearts, that knowing God, in the intimate way suggested by the Bible's carnal analogue, is most of what matters. Not to know God is to be ignorant about the one thing necessary and what makes for peace. It is to have missed one's mark egregiously, and so to have sinned substantially.

I would link this consideration of the knowledge of God to Nelson's arguments for men's acceptance of their mortality. It is knowledge (inseparable from love) of the undying God that can soften the pains of facing up to one's mortality. It is taking to heart the symbolism of the risen Christ that can rob death of its cruel victory. Knowing the living God means knowing why it is reasonable to hope that one will survive the grave. Concomitantly, it is finding a reason to hope that all the precious relationships one developed on earth will be preserved in heaven. The imagery of the book of Revelation that presents heaven as a great chorus of saints engaged ceaselessly in praising God seems to me one of the most precious resources for the Christian imagination. For it, or its equivalents in the other New Testament theologies, not to appear in pastoral treatments of mortality seems deeply regrettable. The one certitude is that we shall die. None of us has seen the imperishable God. We all have to believe that the divine mystery is real, gracious, and so saving. Those of us who are drawn by the evangelical Christ are not spared the need for faith. Far from it. But we are blessed with wonderful human images of how God's will to immortalize human beings works.

There was a human being, like us in all things save sin, who died most cruelly. He had risked everything on his vision of

God, on the hopes God had put in his heart, and his enemies seemed to be triumphing. Only after he had cried out to God his sense of forsakenness and commended to his Father his bruised spirit was his life consummated, and that consummation proved to be only penultimate. Unthinkably, yet for faith completely really, God reached into the bowels of death and drew him forth. Indeed, God set him in heaven, at the Father's right hand, and presented him to the saints as the Lamb slain for their salvation. Seeing this, the saints could only bow low and sing about the worthiness of the Lamb who was slain to receive all honor and power and glory. If that cannot soothe human beings' fears about death, nothing can. What more could God have done? The problem is not the plan of salvation that God conceived from eternity and executed through the flesh of Christ. The problem is our human reluctance to believe that God could be so good. Such reluctance, no doubt rooted in our fears of what such a goodness might demand of us, explains why we run to idols, including world views that focus on just the psychic or just the social. Whenever we do turn from the scenarios of faith, though, we surrender our birthright for a bowl of pottage. God would give us an immortalizing share in the love that moves the stars. Who has offered anything comparable?

To call for men to embrace their masculinity may seem strange, yet Nelson is right to stress the need. Nowadays both men and women are easily confused about their sexual roles, if not their sexual substance, because of the considerable social change wrought in the past generation. The women's movement is the most obvious agent of such change, and feminism the most obvious theoretical product, but this movement has reached into every nook and cranny.[15]

Both men and women now are reluctant to specify particular traits as characteristically masculine or feminine. Both fear stereotypes, yet both also want to be comfortable with the bodies and psyches birth has given them. Women resent being pressured to accept a "masculine" style as they advance in business careers. Many women also resent the ultra-feminization that some feminists seem to hawk as the counterforce such pressuring requires: bracelets up to the elbows, shades of eye shadow found nowhere in nature. Men have similar resentments, most of them perhaps focusing on an irritation that nothing about sexual behavior now is clear. What is courtesy and what is effrontery, what is treating a woman like a woman (and so being condescending) and what is treating a woman like a man (and so being insulting) is never pinned down. Men can feel that women are being capricious, jumping to whichever side of an argument or pique presently pleases them. More significantly, they can feel that they are foolish to get trapped into all such emotional muck and would be better off either keeping quiet or speaking straight, declarative sentences that brook no opposition.

There is, of course, no simple formula that will set the sexes into tidy traffic patterns. The more researchers study how even highly patriarchal, formalized groups in fact have behaved, the more they find that power and influence always overflow the official banks. Regularly the theme is that women's unofficial power has rivaled men's official power. One can claim, as I do, that it would be better to regularize the equality such a state of affairs suggests by making the official power open to qualified women, but even that is not going to settle the matter. For example, ordaining women to the Catholic priesthood, which I favor, is not going to guarantee a faith without problems about sexuality. Men and women are always going to have to negotiate the differences that biology and socializing instill in them. They are always going to have to draw from their common humanity enough mutual respect to keep such differences more enlivening and attractive than destructive. Women are never going to understand men as fully as men would like, and men are never going to understand women as fully as women would like. Their common task, therefore, is to show one another compassion, make themselves quick to offer and ask forgiveness, and constantly remind themselves that, because they don't fully understand, they ought to go gently with one another.

Against this background, I believe that accepting one's masculinity ought to include accepting one's inclination to be strong, take responsibility, hone a lucid mind, develop a warmth that mixes desire and tenderness, and make a virtue of the frequently more limited emotional range that, compared to women, men seem to exhibit. I think that men ought to accept competition, while purifying it of its excesses, that they ought to hold one another to high standards of honor, and that they ought to fight against the clubbiness that either disparages women or colludes in evil. Such evil may be merely the mediocrity one so often finds in bureaucracies, where the combination of orderliness and loyalty can stifle creativity. It may be the cowardice that keeps men from telling the emperor he has no clothes. Or it may be the agreement to a brutality that condones the notion that only the bottom line is important, that "realism" demands the sacrifice of those who can't keep up, or of considerations that challenge the game one's group has constructed, saying that it distorts reality. (I am thinking of the games corporations construct, in which a man's family responsibilities are of virtually no account.)

To accept their masculinity, in its ambiguity, Christian men hardly can do better than to pray about it and discuss it in explicitly religious terms. How ought their love for Christ to shape their sense of being male? What can they draw from the image of God as a father? What does their love of women's beauty suggest about their emotional responses to God? How does the call of Christ to render justice sharpen the challenge to be strong and do what is right?

One scenario, perhaps quite traditional, has men being the solid center, the source of stability around which women can freely play, charm, and create. Another scenario, perhaps equally traditional, has women providing the emotional foundations of a family (the unconditional love children need) and men supplying the rational ordering. Both scenarios obviously have their limitations and often do not render what actually is going on. But each could represent the kind of questions a man wanting to clarify his masculinity might take to Christ. Each could concretize the confusions that gaining a proper understanding of one's ideal masculinity today must dissipate.

I believe that a future spirituality suitable for Christian men must find a way to ease the tensions now attending sexual questions and stimulate more humility and play. I agree with Nelson that giving sexuality a more central and positive role in spirituality is crucial. On the other hand, I see our sexuality as occasioning considerable laughter, when we can approach it without fear. Sex is a funny way to have been constructed—wonderful, immensely pleasurable, yet comic. So much of our humanity comes from our spiritual desires, our angelic ambitions to know and love God precisely as God, that the limitations set by our bodies have to be either tragic or comic.

If we believe that God has created us wisely, we must stress the comic. If we believe that the incarnate Word is God's best and fullest self-expression for human beings, we must stress what helps us to love our flesh, to bless it, to deal with it tenderly and lovingly, as we would with a child or spouse. My own tendency is to work my body until it gives out, and then castigate it as weak, unreliable, not carrying its load. I suspect many men have this tendency, because much in our socializing has made pushing ourselves right and giving in to weakness wrong. Eventually, of course, the body, if not the spirit, teaches us more nuance. The mellowing that comes with middle age may first seem simply no longer having the energy to rage at every injustice, but soon it can shape a view of reality that seems objectively wiser. The more history one learns, the more one contemplates the patience of God. The more one's own impatience seems immature, the more the Spirit may be nigh.

❧ 13 ❧

Persons
or Personality Types?

As I said in previous chapters, an important trend in the developing field of male spirituality is the tendency to turn to psychology for answers and models, especially to Jungian psychology. The Jungian perspective offers significant insights that I find both illuminating and limiting.

What Men Are Like, by John A. Sanford and George Lough, is a recent example of this kind of analysis. From a Jungian standpoint the authors deal with masculine development (boyhood and adolescence), with the tyranny of the ego (a man's need to contact his emotions), how work figures in men's psychology, what tends to happen to men in midlife, men's relationships (as friends, lovers, fathers, sons), men's sexual fantasies, how old age can crystallize the process of individuation (finding or making one's self), and how the anima (the feminine side of the male psyche) functions in dreams, fairy tales, and myths. Two appendixes treat the Jungian typology of personalties and adolescent development as illustrated in Lewis Carroll's *Alice in Wonderland*. The general result is a rich, if leisurely and seldom profound, discussion of male psychology.

For my interests in men's spirituality, the main benefits of *What Men Are Like* is its stimulus to think about men's fantasies, interactions with women, and problems in gaining a sense of wholeness. To take these in reverse order, I would first note that all human beings have to grow toward wholeness. Women no less than men have to keep striving, if they are one day to feel that their various personality traits flow from an integral self. If women typically have fewer problems integrating mind and heart, they also typically have more problems achieving an independent self and fashioning a pathway to meet their own distinctive needs. Men's drive to find such a pathway can keep them from establishing warm contacts with a wide variety of people, and it can make them strangers to their own interiority (their feelings and deepest thoughts) until they enter the second half of their lifecycles.

Sanford and Lough advise men to get in touch with their psyches, especially their feminine sides, either by introspection or through counseling. My reaction is that while such advice is sound enough, it is somewhat obviated when men pray contemplatively and inform themselves about traditional Christian spirituality. As well, such advice does not touch on the deeper question: What is an integral self for? Unless gaining individuation is an end in itself, the Augustinian proposition that God has made us for himself remains in full force. The advantage of traditional Christian instruction in spiritual reading, contemplative prayer, confession, is that it deals with both integration and finality. That is, one attending to Thomas à Kempis, *The Cloud of Unknowing*, Ignatius Loyola, John of the Cross, or similar masters learns that the heart is more important than the head, that the key thing is to attend to God in love, that darkness often is more profound than light, that evangelical images must be handled poetically, and that the Spirit is the only adequate teacher of prayer. One also learns that knowing, loving, and serving God is the reason human beings have been given life, and that often God is best loved and served by attending to one's neighbors. For both the integration proposed by the traditional masters and the service of God, Christ stands forth as the nonpareil exemplar. Thus à Kempis spoke of the imitation of Christ and Loyola taught people to ask to be with Christ under the banner of the cross.

Concerning men's relations with women, *What Men Are Like* is especially helpful in locating the psychological roots of many of the misperceptions of women to which men are prone. Whether or not one accepts the full Jungian theory of anima and animus, it seems undeniable that many men, on meeting an attractive woman, idealize her by projecting onto her traits that stem as much from their own inner desires as from the woman's actual characteristics. Thus it is commonplace for men to find a women extraordinary on first meeting and quite ordinary on fifth meeting. Presumably something much the same occurs with women meeting men. To what extent men are in fact romancing their own feminine side (anima) and women are romancing their own masculine side (animus) is hard for me to say. At times Sanford and Lough write as though there were no flesh and blood, objective other in the picture, only a projection of one's own psychic needs or desires. But the warning to beware of romantic first impressions, and strive to let the other person be what he or she actually is, is well taken. The greater a person's hunger for love and affirmation, the more strongly this warning ought to echo.

In this psychological approach to men's dealings with women, I find considerable intrigue but little actual eros. The stress on the subjective components of the male mental world seems to tame the outgoing drive of eros, which typically wants to gain the beauty and goodness of the other. Whether this other be a fine woman or God, it deflates and shrivels if one is making it more the occasion for self-discovery than the occasion for forgetting self and seeking ecstatic union. No doubt we never are so

pure in our dealings with either other people or God that we
aren't also enjoying the self-knowledge or self-approbation that
successful dealings tend to entail. But what Eric Voegelin, following Henri Bergson, called the "open soul" (the soul rightly
ordered) keeps first things first. First is the objective goodness of
the other, to which one goes out in acts of self-transcendence.
First is the need of the other, to which one goes out in acts of
compassion and care. Genuine love involves forgetting self,
leaving selfishness and self-concern behind. Like a miracle, the
young woman who was self-absorbed can lose herself in devotion to her baby or her husband. The same with the young man
who finds a lover, or a cause, or a child dominating his horizon
and giving him something much better than self-concern upon
which to lavish his attention.

Men's fantasies seem to involve much sexual content, and
What Men Are Like joins with Nelson's book, *The Intimate Connection,* in suggesting that we deal with this both positively and
matter-of-factly, with none of the fear or condemnation that religion has tended to show sex in the past. Despite a lengthy
chapter on the subject, however, the book does little to explain
where this great sexual interest comes from, leaving one to conjecture that hormones, or perhaps the psyche's searches for
wholeness, are the source. I would postulate inspirations of the
Spirit, departing from much of the Christian spiritual tradition,
which generally viewed sexual fantasies as temptations. Inasmuch as they can make one narcissistic or auto-erotic, they certainly can be temptations, invitations to back away from self-
transcendence, objectivity, and a love in which the spirit is more
powerful than the flesh. On the other hand, sexual fantasies can
tell us a great deal about what we desire in a lover, as well as a
great deal about what is comic in being embodied.

The man who fancies himself in possession of a harem, with
which he performs prodigious sexual feats, might turn aside to
God, that they both could enjoy a good laugh. He might thank
God for letting him feel a moment of vigor in which he could
imagine being up to such a pleasurable task, likening that feeling to those he used to have when playing ball in the back yard.

Then his fantasy was to strike out the side in the ninth inning of the World Series. Even as a boy he knew that was unlikely to happen, yet picturing it gave him a relatively innocent pleasure and allowed him to feel good about himself. So with many male sexual fantasies. If a man finds himself imagining a beautiful woman stimulating him to wit, chivalry, strength, sexual skill, and the like, he can return to his relations with real women both challenged and encouraged. Of course he will discover that real interactions with women differ from his fantasies as much as his actual performance for his little league baseball team differed from his fantasy about the World Series. But without some imagination, he probably won't have the wit to be playful with women, nor have the self-deprecating humor often necessary to be attractive. Naturally, fantasies that run toward brutality or gross selfishness are more harmful than helpful. Naturally, women have the right to be treated as real people, rather than as whores or madonnas. But fantasy that provides amusement and recreation, helping men return to the worlds of work and social interactions with more bounce in their stride, ought to be encouraged. If male sexual fantasies are as inevitable as Sanford and Lough suggest, it is far better to guide them toward a positive use than to repress them and risk their decaying in the psychic underground.

What Men Are Like offers some delightful and insightful interpretations of fairy tales, especially those from the Arthurian cycle. The point seems to be reading such stories as that of Sir Gawain and the Green Knight as symbolic expressions of the stages men must go through, if they are to gain the maturity of individuation. Such a maturity seems to emerge as what developmental psychologists sketch: a proper balance between autonomy and the ability to relate to others, a proper balance between reason and feeling, an ability to drive hard for success, yet let go and enjoy wider perspectives when success threatens to become idolatrous.

In profiting from a Jungian interpretation of fairy tales, I am reminded of the benefits that insight can bring. Even when the yield of one's studies is only hypotheses—patterns that might illumine the data—one's world has expanded, one's sense of one's possibilities has grown, and so one has beamed. We take great delight in glimpsing new realms of meaning. The beauty and order that insights bring is one of the primal joys of human existence. Not to praise a system, psychological or other, that helped one to such joy would be mean-spirited and ungrateful. If pastoral theologians and counselors are turning to psychological studies because they have found them capable of illumining the dynamics of people's images and feelings, and so capable of bringing considerable expansion of people's horizons, one can only second their efforts.

It remains to be said, however, that some insights are more profound or comprehensive than others. Having taken to heart the lessons so artfully expressed in the tale of Sir Gawain and the Green Knight (and having reminded oneself that no theory ever exhausts a classical piece of art or can substitute for its marriage of particular details and generalizing illuminations), the theologian yet can, must, ask about the consequences for salvation or divinization. How does the insight gained about the maturation of the male psyche contribute to the strength that psyche needs to die well? "Quite directly," a psychologist might say, arguing that they end best who have run well in the middle of the course. Granted, yet it remains true that the end is not simply more of the middle. The end, in Christian perspective, really is an end. Death and eternity are not simply prolongations of what went before. The gospels hint at this when they depict the risen Christ as both like, and unlike, the Jesus the disciples knew before the crucifixion.

One could argue for the necessity for theology from the beginning, as well as from the end, but let us content ourselves with the end. For Christian faith, something definitive attaches to Christian death. One is not simply exiting in order to start another phase of the karmic cycle. One is not simply leaving to join the world of universal archetypes. The myth of the eternal return, which made so many ancient cultures picture time as an endless circle, has been shattered by the Logos of God. Once and for all, Christ died and rose, beginning a new eon of human existence. Taken into the Father's eternity, he was the first of many brothers and sisters God has wanted to immortalize similarly. So what the good race of the middle years, the good works of individuation and psychic maturation, are preparing for, willy-nilly, is an encounter with judgment and eternity. "Judgment," far from being mainly negative, is another mercy of God. Without it there would be no separation of good and evil, no resolution of the ambiguities always attaching to time, no victory of Christ the new Adam, no dismissal of death and injustice as merely intermediary things.

What might the contemplation of these convictions of Christian faith import into the development of the male personality? Considerably broadened and deepened perspectives, and considerably more hope. If men, and of course women, at bottom yearn for the triumph of light over darkness, of love over hate, then the eschatological assurances of Christianity are at the core of the salvation for which men are hungering. Such assurances say that the game does end, the issue finally is settled, men do not have to struggle forever, and they are granted an outcome. Thus, men and women do not live in a world of absurdity, a world with no definitive outcomes. Equally, they do not live in a world in which everything is permitted (the moral ambiguity that prefigures the hell of definitive absurdity).

Now, some religious systems (for example, the Hindu and the Chinese), some psychologies (for example, the Jungian) and some feminist theories (for example, those rooted in Celtic witchcraft) have argued for the bi-polarity of good and evil, the naturalness of darkness always shadowing light, of death always infiltrating life. To their mind, the dichotomies and definitive solutions of biblical religion (or of the theologies rooted in biblical religion) shortchange reality, play false to the complexity and dualism built into the universe, and so have injured people's psyches or retarded their resignation. The problem I see with this position is that it makes the finitude and complexity of the natural and human worlds absolute, denying that divinity might be radically other.

One finds this tendency, as well, in process theology, a bequest of Alfred North Whitehead that lately has attracted many feminist theologians and so complicated (or enriched) discussions of a spirituality for sexual equals. The divinity developed in process theology by and large cannot deliver the salvation promised in Christian revelation. The divinity of process theology is dynamic—attractively so—but in consequence limited. It can intend the triumph of good over evil but it cannot assure that triumph. So the process theologians' interpretation of the Incarnation of the Logos cannot be that of John's gospel, which makes the Word's taking flesh the dawn of the eschatological age and definitive salvation. Their interpretation of the resurrection cannot agree with that of Saint Paul, who saw it as a new creation. All must be shaped to the dualism, the both/and, of human experience. The reaches of human imagination and judgment toward something radically transcendent, radically simple, radically other have to be denied.

This poses a tough methodological problem, with implications for spirituality, because even those arguing for radical otherness have to do so with human images and concepts. The traditional Catholic love for analogy helps to some degree, yet even analogy cannot bear the full weight of what the Spirit seems to be inspiring at the roots of the personality, where faith, hope, and love bear interest on a down payment of divine life. So one has to head into the *via negativa*, the mystagogy that firms up one's convictions that the radical otherness of God is an equally radical immanence and functions as the original blessing that warms creation from within.

How to render such poetic language in more rigorous terms is a good question. Perhaps we should say that what is experienced in naked prayer grounds an ontology in which rest has rights equal to those of process. To be sure, Whitehead spoke of a polarity in God, to account for both rest and process. But he did not make such rest or removal from change and suffering the paramount experience directing his theological predication.

The objective immortality that Whitehead intuited sits awkwardly astride the constant change of the divinity at work suffering in the world to suggest (not accomplish) the world's salvation. Jesus is not the focus of an immortalization which is the consequence of a yes to the personal divine love and so an acceptance of the personal aseity, the personal self-sufficiency that for the Christian philosopher makes God God. In a word, one has only half the biblical world view: the motion, the engagement of God with the world, but not the rest, not the divine Sabbath spoken of in Hebrews. Thus one has only half a loaf, and so a diminished spirituality. For unless one's labors alongside God take one, in deep prayer and at death, into the limitless *tota simul* (eternity) of God, divinization on the biblical model has not occurred. The Spirit in whom the Johannine theology has counseled one to abide has not been making one a partaker of the trinitarian substance. The Spirit and the Son have not been leading one into the endless depths of the divine Father, the eternal unbegotten.

It is true that this theological language remains limited, partial, indebted to human experience and thus to change and mortality. It is true that even its negatives, its alpha privatives, do not capture the mystery of God. But they do point to a salvation transcending the wholeness of the psyche, and they do conjure the peace and joy of hoping for what eye has not seen and ear has not heard, what it has not entered the heart of human beings to conceive: what God has prepared for those who love God and let themselves trust that the Spirit is more real than the self it keeps in being and faith.

What Men Are Like closes with an appendix describing the eight fundamental personalities that Jungian psychology has found to be typical of the general range that people manifest. These eight fundamental personality types are multiples of two categories and four functions. The two categories are introvert and extrovert. For Jung, people divided into those whose instincts took them outward and those whose instincts took them inward. The four functions are thinking, feeling, sensing, and intuition. By marrying one's predominant category to one's predominant function, one can find one's basic personality type. For example, one might study one's inclinations and decide that one is an extroverted feeling type, or an introverted thinking type. Devising, administering, and interpreting tests that show one's personality type (according to this Jungian scheme) has become a substantial business.

My reaction to this typology is parallel to my reaction to the analysis of fairy tales (or dreams) according to Jungian (or Freudian, or other) theories of how the psyche labors to produce mental health. Inasmuch as the typology provides some illuminating hypotheses about a given person's natural inclinations, and so suggests what sort of work he or she might find most congenial, it seems a useful tool, something to commend. Insight of any substantial sort is a gracious gift, and if we must always test our hypotheses (recognize the difference between insight and judgment), that does not discredit hypotheses themselves. When Bernard Lonergan said that insights are a dime a dozen, he did not mean to throw cold water on the flash of light in which they arise. Far from it. He simply wanted to indicate that only the hypotheses that we verify provide us a solid foundation, whether in science or in daily life. The question for the psychological tests and their interpreters therefore is whether in fact they guide one toward a better self-understanding and line of work. The question for the theologian interested in personality types as an aspect of a spirituality for men is how they color the fundamental task of growing to the measure Christ has in mind.

I have always been frustrated by psychological tests, because I have always felt that the choices the tests asked me to make were false. Granted, my experience with such tests has been limited, but the ones I have seen take the form of "Would you rather do A or B?" Well, sometimes I would rather read a book and sometimes I would rather swim a mile. Sometimes I would like to go to a party, eat some pizza, drink some beer, and sometimes I would like to be alone with my word processor, or alone in a dark and quiet chapel, or alone walking the beach. Indeed, sometimes I would like to be walking alone (collectedly) with another, my wife or a good friend. Sometimes I would like to be connected to others in silence, as at the peak of a liturgy or in a circle of prayer. I tend to like art (music, painting) more than science, but at times biology and mathematics have shocked me by their complex beauty. I tend to think politics a sweaty, impure affair, but at times I've marveled at the skill that gaining consensus demands. I hate to travel, yet I love to go to new places, to be forced to reshuffle my images. I want an early retirement, yet I cannot conceive of not working for more than two weeks. And so it goes. Anything so dichotomous as "Would you rather do A or B" distorts the personality and world I know from first hand experience. Anything dichotomizing the world into the chaste and the sexy, the ascetic and the gourmand, loses my trust.

I doubt that my reaction is idiosyncratic, and I suspect that it implies more than the lack of sophistication that popular testing to date has achieved. First, it clearly suggests that many people have personalities with major and minor chords. I may be primarily an introvert but much in me responds to extroversion. I don't know whether thinking or feeling is my predominant mode, but I'm fairly sure it is not sensing. Still, when prodded by a Beethoven sonata or a whimsical painting of Chagall, I become a very acute listener, a very careful viewer. So any test hoping to earn my trust has to give me results that are subtly shaded. Presumably, it also would have to give me practical advice similarly subtly shaded.

Second, I think that the subtleties of our shaded personalities probably find an exact reflection in the varieties of our prayer. I have been thrilled by a Gregorian Mass and warmed by a silent, Quaker-like prayer circle. I have loved contemplating a Byzantine ikon yet loved even more the dark velvet prayer that uses no images. Reading the gospels and other good books has been greatly nourishing, but so has watching the stars move across a black, frigid sky over the Grand Tetons. And surely others more faithful to prayer, more energetic in searching out sources of growth in intimacy with God, can report a much richer repertoire. Each of the "methods" of prayer, Western or Eastern, that would come to mind in an academic inventory—Hasidic, Sufi, Yogic, Shamanic, and much more—has its logic and wisdom. Yet each also suggests the Christian instinct that finally the Holy

Spirit is the master of prayer, shaping what is traditional to the needs of one's psyche.

To appreciate the Holy Spirit, I suspect, some learning about the experience of one's betters with prayer is desirable, but not the bottom line. The Spirit usually does not leap over the stages of ordinary human growth, which require enriching one's experience and sifting it through trial and error. On the other hand, the Spirit seems to grow impatient with the heady aspects of prayer and rather quickly to demand attention, focus, concentration from the heart. Thus, with some fear and trembling, as well as much indolence, I have put my money on emptying my mind and trying to direct my heart toward the blank fullness of God. Often, indeed usually, this has gone badly, and one of my greatest embarrassments has been the increase, rather than the decrease, of distractions. On the other hand, when I have tried returning to books or images or verbal formulas, they have only given limited, temporary satisfaction. So I have gratefully seized on essays that suggested that one ought to pray when and as one feels inclined, all the while thinking it important to have a regular time for prayer each day, to remind myself of my debts to the Spirit.

The point is not my own predilections but my suspicion that the Spirit deals with all of us individually. We are not one of eight types, even when we find some help by locating ourselves in a given combination of category and function. We are each a potential dear to God, who easily creates freshly and beautifully. It is no problem for God to deal with five billion unique personalities. God does not need eight classifications to simplify the work of sanctification.

✆ 14 ✆

Conclusion

I REMEMBER HEARING A FRIEND SOME some years older than I say that he, a nuclear engineer, was surprised to find how much he was enjoying reading history. Lately I've been feeling the same way, though perhaps for a different reason. The more I've learned about other eras and cultures, the more I've felt liberated from restrictive interpretations of "orthodoxy." One certainly can find lessons about the necessity of the middle way between an individual inspiration that despises community controls and community controls that stifle individual inspiration. But few other lessons impose certainty. Indeed, the more that historians broaden the range of their data, so that their plot-lines are not limited to what the rich, the powerful, the males, the racially predominant were doing, the more one realizes that nobody knows precisely what contours the past assumed. Nobody has a God's-eye view. The only certainty is that the full actuality spills out of all the containers we have poured it into.

Now, if nobody knows the past with certitude, all the more can we say that nobody knows the present or the future. Wisdom therefore must consist in making a virtue of nescience. Wisdom must incline people to saying, with Socrates, that they are only proud that they realized they didn't know and stopped deceiving themselves (and others). Wisdom must be reminiscent of Karl Rahner's notion that, for times so complex as today's, the prime task of pastoral theology is not to run breathlessly, trying to keep up with each new advance in scientific or humanistic knowledge, but to contemplate the heart of the matter and proffer short formulas of Christian faith.

What are the bedrock verities that ought to figure in such formulas? By my reckoning, they include human mortality (we all die), human ignorance (none of us ever knows everything relevant, all of us must take the risk of faith), the transcendence of God (what we cannot know or do, God perhaps can), and the adequacy of Jesus Christ (everything essential to salvation and wisdom is manifest in him; he is God's sufficient response to the question, the hunger for meaning, constituting our human nature).

We all die. Although our culture tries to distract us from this bedrock fact, it remains a great source of wisdom. Does anything mortal deserve our full allegiance? Does not mortality (which extends from our flesh to many of our cultural products) cut the legs out from under idolatry? When will we learn what the Bible means when it tells us not to put our trust in princes? When will masculinity come to reside more in wisdom and goodness than in sports, politics, warfare, power, wealth, or fame? Will masculinity one day spotlight compassion for all who have to die, because men have seen the implications of the fear and trembling mortality easily brings?

Second, we are all ignorant. Compared to what there is to know, we all fall so far short that our pretensions are ludicrous.

Wise people would immediately translate this realization into a humble, humorous style of speaking. People in the know would most treasure those willing to discuss how they have coped with their ignorance, what sort of Socratic proceeding they have found most helpful. People of faith would intuit how human ignorance is a fine springboard to petition of God, even as they would realize how easily such a spiritual movement can abdicate human responsibility. We can all learn many useful things, and our world ought to be much less polluted, much more just, much more beautiful than it is. The presence or absence of human intelligence has a great deal to do with the quotients of suffering human beings have to endure. Nonetheless, at the truly bottom line, where theology ought often to take up residence, our mouths are stopped and we can only beg God for help. Wise are we if we visit that bottom line frequently.

Third, God is truly transcendent, truly a fullness not limited by mortality and ignorance as we are. God's transcendence also exceeds our sin, and so even when our hearts condemn us God is not defeated. Usually we shortchange God, not having taken the divine transcendence to heart. Usually we consider God's residence in our hearts, through grace, something esoteric or so hard to tie down with experiential terms that it should not figure in spiritual counsel. The truth, of course, is just the opposite. The truth is that nothing is more relevant than the presence of God in our hearts, because in the spiritual life all the priority resides with God. We cannot think about anything apart from the divine transcendence, the divine immensity that provides our thought its backdrop and horizon. We cannot love anything apart from the being of God that gives everything the context of its goodness. Every bit of courage, hope, trust, love that bubbles up in our hearts depends on the Spirit who brooded over creation and holds us in grace. God is more intimate to us than we are to ourselves, God is more who and what we are than we are ourselves. Everything positive in us comes from God. We are God limited by a body, a finite spirit, a sinful heart, a given culture and historical period. All of these limitations naturally mean that we are not God. But the being they stop, the love and creativity they channel, comes from God, in a real sense is God. None of this had to be. God need not have made us. Having made us, God need not have saved us and taken up so intimate a residence in us that what God has always been (perfect knowing and loving) now is our core, the best of us.

Last, the adequacy of Christ ought to make men stay, abide, in the biblical images, the traditional teachings, and above all the current prayer that brings Christ alive for them. In himself Christ is always alive, the risen Lord, the quickened spirit, the head of his Body. For us, Christ is bound to be the prophet and healer from Nazareth, who showed how simple yet amazing humanity could be. We ought never to wander far from the flashing fire of the risen, apocalyptic Christ, who is the victor over death and holds the keys to life and heaven.

Still, probably the suffering, crucified Christ, fulfilling the servant songs of Isaiah, is more constantly relevant. As we hurt, move into deeper darkness, worry about our children, lose our strength, and feel our faith attacked, the passible, mortal Jesus can increasingly show us the mercy of God. Who could have thought that God would have not only known but loved our need so profoundly that God would become one of us and show how that need can be borne, succored, transformed into a claim upon nothing less than a parental divine love? Who could have expected that God would find a way to make nothing human in us foreign to the divine experience? Our sin, which separates us from Christ, finally becomes our greatest claim upon him. When he said that his revelations made his disciples not servants but friends, he invited all drawn by his beauty to open their hearts and confess their sins without restraint. Seventy times seven the forgiveness of Christ resounds. To please him, we have only to go and do likewise, never casting the first stone, always remembering God loved us before we were worthy—indeed, remembering that we never shall be worthy.

Christian spirituality, for men or women, is never about worthiness. Always it is about grace. What God has done in creation, salvation, and divinization is always undeserved. At all times the proper attitude is thanksgiving and wonder that

God could be so good. Compared to the goodness of God, the follies, even the evils, of human beings are at best secondary. In fact, only the goodness of God shows the proper significance of human folly and evil. The greatest sign of original sin, I have come to think, is our having so often had the experience, been given the data, of the divine goodness and missed the meaning. The spirituality for men that I am most interested in helping develop pivots on such meaning. What we see in a glass darkly, and hope one day to understand face to face, is the wisdom, perhaps the inevitability, of God's having always dealt with us and our world purely from love.

Notes

1. See John Carmody, *The Heart of the Christian Matter* (Nashville: Abingdon, 1983); *Holistic Spirituality* (New York: Paulist, 1983).

2. I have also been ambivalent about the topic of a spirituality for men, and its correlative, a spirituality for women, because it has seemed inevitably to raise the question of homosexuality. I do not want to have always to qualify what I am describing and make the distinctions gay men and women rightly can ask for, so let me say once and for all that I think some people have an unchangeably homosexual orientation, that this is part of their endowment from God, and that both they and any community they inhabit are healthier when this is as overt a part of their profile as their ethnic origins, their job skills, or their sense of humor. I think homosexuals are held to the same general morality as heterosexuals, that this morality boils down to honesty and love, and that genuinely homosexual relationships should neither bear any special restrictions nor claim any special exemptions.

From 1963 to 1966, I watched a young counselee and friend struggle to find himself and God. He succeeded only when he owned up to what he knew he was and took a wry pride in it. Six years ago he died of AIDS. I cannot bring him back to accept my apologies for the inadequacies of my counsel and friendship, nor to help him criticize his interpretation of his homosexuality. But, I can come out of the closet about what I think Christian faith should say about homosexuality. In Saint Teresa's words, it should say let nothing disturb you. In Saint Augustine's words, it should say love and do what you will. I believe this advice, and all the other essentials of the Christian life, apply equally to men and women, to heterosexuals and homosexuals, to blacks and whites, to rich and poor. It leaves many further questions unanswered, of course, but it offers all people the evangelical bottom line: God is greater than our hearts, God is love.

3. Barry Lopez, *Arctic Dreams* (New York: Charles Scribner's Sons, 1986), p. xx.

4. See James V. Schall, *The Distinctiveness of Christianity* (San Francisco: Ignatius, 1982).

5. See Avery Dulles, *A Church to Believe In* (New York: Crossroad, 1983).

6. See Lucas Grollenberg, *Jesus* (Philadelphia: Westminster, 1978).

7. See James D. G. Dunn, *Jesus and the Spirit* (Philadelphia: Westminster, 1975).

8. See Mary Field Belenky *et al., Women's Ways of Knowing* (New York: Basic Books, 1986).

9. For example, the participants in the symposium on the state of American Catholicism published in the March, 1987, issue of New Oxford Review seem unconscionably insular. First, one notes that all eleven of them are men. Someone, presumably the organizer of the symposium for NOR, has an impossibly narrow view of American church membership. In less benign interpretation, someone sensed that the most volatile issues in the American church swirl around the status of women and so deliberately tilted the game. Second, I noted that these eleven men egregiously ignored what I, following Karl Rahner, would call the cardinal mysteries of Christian faith. Compared to the time the authors spent on abortion, Roman authority, obedience, the pros and cons of dissent, the accommodation to paganism, and other supposed peculiarities of American Catholicism, the time spent on Trinity, Grace, and Incarnation was scandalously miniscule. After reading these fairly representative pundits, I seriously doubted they had much understanding of Catholic Christianity.

10. See Charles E. Curran, *Faithful Dissent* (Kansas City: Sheed and Ward, 1986).

11. Martin W. Pable, O.F.M. Cap., *A Man and His God* (Notre Dame, Ind.: Ave Maria, 1988); James B. Nelson, *The Intimate Connection* (Philadelphia: Westminster, 1988); John A. Sanford and George Lough, *What Men Are Like* (New York: Paulist Press, 1988).

12. Pable, *A Man and His God*, p. 121.

13. See John Carmody, *Holistic Spirituality.*

14. Nelson, *The Intimate Connection*, pp. 13-14.

15. See, for example, ed. Alice Jardine and Paul Smith, *Men in Feminism* (New York: Methuen, 1987).